HAUNTED BURLINGTON, WISCONSIN

MARY SUTHERLAND

Forewords by Linda Godfrey & Frank Joseph

Haunted
America

Published by Haunted America
A Division of The History Press
Charleston, SC 29403
www.historypress.net

First published 2014

Manufactured in the United States

ISBN 978.1.62619.321.5

Library of Congress CIP data applied for.

By stepping outside the box and believing—not in what society tells you, but your heart—you become the hero of your own journey.
—Mary Sutherland

Acknowledgement
A special thank-you to all my family and friends who have followed me on my journey investigating the mysteries of Burlington.

CONTENTS

DEDICATION

G enetic memory is invoked to explain the racial memory postulated by Carl Jung. In Jungian psychology, racial memories are posited memories, feelings and ideas inherited from our ancestors as part of a "collective unconscious."

This book is dedicated to my great-great-grandmother Nan'yehi, known in English as Nancy Ward, the last Beloved Woman of the Cherokees. I truly believe it is from my cell memories and the blood that connects us two that I gravitate toward the traditions and beliefs of my ancient ancestors. The ancient countries of the region lie between southern Appalachia and Arkansas. Here are found mounds, inscribed tablets, sculptures, sacred pipes and shell ornaments. This is the home of the ancient temples and mound builders, the Etowah, Adena and Cahokia. The land and DNA are my links to the Cherokee tradition of the Beloved Woman, or War Woman (*Ghigua*), Nan'yehi.

Nan'yehi is the most famous of the Cherokee Beloved Women, whose roles were the highest Cherokee women could aspire to. The title *Ghigua* Nan'yehi earned while leading her people, after her husband was mortally wounded, to victory during a battle against the Creeks.

In her role as Beloved Woman, Nan'yehi performed such duties as sitting in General Council (where she had full voice and voting power), heading the Women's Council, preparing the Black Drink for the Green Corn Ceremony and acting as a negotiator in treaty parlays. It is noted that in meeting with John Sevier to strike peace terms with the Americans at Little

Pigeon River, Tennessee, in 1781, she was appalled that he had brought no female negotiators. He was equally appalled that she was trusted with such an important task. It has been recorded that she sent him back to his people stating her terms: "Let your women hear our words."

Nan'yehi is credited for stopping Toqua's warriors from burning Lydia Bean at the stake. Bean, the wife of Tennessee's first permanent settler, was forced to stay at the home of Nan'yehi before returning to Watauga. Taking advantage of Bean's stay, Nan'yehi learned the art of making butter and cheese, subsequently purchasing cattle and introducing dairying to the Cherokee people.

She participated in several treaty negotiations and even spoke at the Treaty of Hopewell in 1785, when she made a dramatic plea for continued peace. At the close of the ceremonies, she invited the commissioners to smoke her pipe of peace and friendship. Nan'yehi looked to the protection of Congress to prevent future disturbances and expressed the hope that the "chain of friendship [would] never be broken." Although the commissioners promised that all settlers would leave Cherokee lands within six months, the whites ignored the treaty, which forced the Cherokee to make additional land cessions.

During the 1790s, Nan'yehi observed enormous changes taking place within the Cherokee Nation. Her people adopted the commercial agricultural lifestyle of the nearby settlers and pressed for a republican form of government. Unlike the old system of clan and tribal loyalty, the new Cherokee government provided no place for a Beloved Woman, thus leaving Nan'yehi, or Nancy Ward, the last of the Beloved Women.

Nancy Ward was born in 1738 at Chota, the sacred "Mother Town" of the Cherokee. The name of her father is not known because the Cherokee society was matrilineal so lineage was only tracked through the female line. Nan'yehi's mother was Tame Doe of the Wolf Clan, the sister of Attakullakulla, civil chief of the Cherokee Nation.

The Hiwassee Purchase of 1819 forced Nan'yehi to abandon Chota. She moved south and settled on the Ocoee River near present-day Benton. There she operated an inn on the Federal Road until her death in 1822.

She was baptized on July 13, 1940, and endowed into the Mormon Salt Lake Temple on November 12, 1940. Of interest to me was the July 13 date; my birthdate is also July 13.

According to the president of the Nancy Ward Society, Nan'yehi had three children: two by her first Cherokee husband (Tsu-la, or Kingfisher) and a daughter by her second husband, Bryan Ward. Their daughter, Elizabeth, was born in 1759 at the Cherokee Nation, now Tennessee. Ward deserted the two and returned to South Carolina to live with his white family. Elizabeth later went on to marry and have children by Joseph Martin, who was the son of Joseph Martin and Susannah Childs. It was through the Childs/Nan'yehi blood that I inherited the Nan'yehi lineage.

As the story goes, General Joseph Martin, from Virginia, was appointed the Indian agent to the Cherokee. Having much in common with Bryan Ward, Joseph and Bryan became close friends. On one of Martin's trips into upper South Carolina, he met Nancy Ward and her daughter Elizabeth. He was entranced by Elizabeth's beauty and asked for her hand in marriage, which was granted. He and Elizabeth purchased land adjacent to Bryan Ward, settling on the west branch of the Toogaloo River in Northeast Georgia, an area that later became Franklin County.

Not much is known about the history, but I was able to find the following reference to hard times during 1782 from an excerpt of the Draper Manuscript: "Things were so bad in the Overhill settlement that in the fall of 1782 Joseph Martin took Nancy Ward and Chief Oconostota back to Long Island to spend the winter. Scarcity of food and respect for Nancy, as well as friendship for the Old Chief who was now almost blind, were sufficient reasons."

Draper's manuscript records this quote from William Martin, son of Joseph: "I am of the opinion that Oconostota was one of the noblest and best of humankind. He had a powerful frame, and in his prime must have weighed more than two hundred pounds, with a head of enormous size. He was, when I saw him, very lean, stooped, and emaciated."

Following the death of his cousin Attacullacula, Oconostota became the great chief of the Cherokee Nation. In 1730, Oconostota was one of six Cherokee delegates who visited England. It was there that he first met one of his future wives, Lucy Ward, who was a lady-in-waiting to the queen. He made a return trip with two other Cherokee in 1762 to meet King George III.

These two Cherokee greats, Nancy Ward and Oconostota, spent the winter of 1782–83 in Joseph Martin's Long Island home, where Nancy's daughter Betsy was able to care for their needs. With the coming of spring, Oconostota asked Martin to take him home. The old chief must have felt that his end was near, and he wanted to spend his last days at Chota. Martin realized that the ailing chief would be unable to make the trip on horseback, so he arranged to take the party downriver by boat. Sometime later, when the veteran chief breathed his last breath, Martin buried the old chief with Christian rites, using a dugout canoe for a coffin.

Nancy Ward was later buried on a nearby hill beside the graves of her son Five Killer and her brother Long Fellow, also known as the Raven. Many honors have been bestowed in her name since her death. Among these, the Nashville, Tennessee chapter of the Daughters of the American Revolution is named for her. A monument was erected on her grave in 1923 by the Nancy Ward Chapter, Daughters of the American Revolution.

FOREWORD

There's something about Burlington: whether it's the way it snuggles around the Fox and White Rivers, its status as a major site of ancient effigy mounds or something yet undiscovered is hard to say, but it's definitely a town where all forms of the strange and unusual seem to thrive. Its long history of hauntings, eccentric people and curious happenings deserves documentation, and I can think of no one more appropriate to host a literary tour of Burlington's weird side than longtime resident Mary Sutherland. Sutherland is not simply a reporter of all these phenomena; she lives them.

Presently best known as co-proprietor (with husband Brad) of the Sci-Fi Café and Research Center, Sutherland has spent two decades poking and prodding into the current and past mysteries of Burlington. The former hotel that houses her business is a perfect microcosm of her studies. The historic building features a sealed entrance to an old tunnel system in its basement, a mother and child ghost duo that seem to appreciate the tune "You Are My Sunshine" and a spirit that makes its presence known by whistling. Former inhabitants of the building have verified that the structure hosted ghosts, secret rooms and scary "shadow people" long before the Sutherlands owned it.

As readers should expect, Mary's studies extend beyond her own experiences. The author and investigator often takes visitors on tours of a park area she believes contains an inter-dimensional vortex (woe to those who bring the wrong "treats" to the resident vortex fairies) and hosts a yearly vortex conference with many well-known speakers on anomalous phenomena. She has searched early newspapers and historical volumes to examine events long forgotten by most of the town's populace, from the esoteric symbols she's documented on older downtown buildings to the remnants of the once thriving Strangite Mormon settlement just outside town. In short, if something floats, morphs or dematerializes in Burlington, Sutherland probably knows about it and has likely included it in this book.

What differentiates *Haunted Burlington, Wisconsin*, from most tomes on haunted locations is that Sutherland includes her explanations of the unknown realms and phenomena with tips for heightening the reader's own psychic awareness. Readers who complete this dizzying journey may find they can no longer look at the lovely little city of Burlington in exactly the same way. Perhaps, then, this book itself may be considered a vortex. And whether or not it actually transports you to another place, it will certainly draw you in.

—Linda Godfrey

Linda S. Godfrey is the award-winning author of over a dozen nonfiction books on strange creatures, people and places and recently released her debut paranormal/urban fantasy, God Johnson: The Unforgiven Diary of the Disciple of a Lesser God, *as a self-published e-book, the first in a series. Godfrey is also an artist and illustrator and a former newspaper reporter. She has been a featured guest on dozens of national TV and radio shows, including* Monsterquest, Sean Hannity's America, Lost Tapes, Inside Edition, *Sy-Fy's* Haunted Highway, Monsters and Mysteries, *Wisconsin and Michigan Public Radio, Coast to Coast AM radio and many more. She and her husband live on the edge of Southeast Wisconsin's Kettle Moraine State Forest along with their Lhasa apso, Grendal. Her latest nonfiction book,* American Monsters: A History of Monster Lore, Legends, and Sightings *in America will be released in August 2014 by Tarcher/Penguin. http://lindagodfrey.com.*

FOREWORD

There are rare persons in this world who see things others don't, persons who connect the dots of existence and possess an instinctive talent for linking with kindred souls to reveal otherwise invisible patterns and excavate hidden truths. Such a person is Mary Sutherland. She is a natural-born networker in all she does—from her Burlington vortex conferences and Sci-Fi Café to her public talks and published books.

—Frank Joseph

Frank Joseph was nominated by Japan's Savant Society as professor of world archaeology. He was editor in chief of Ancient American Magazine *from 1993 to 2007 and has traveled the world collecting research materials for his twenty-seven published books.*

INTRODUCTION

In the late 1980s and early '90s, while living in Phoenix, Arizona, I maintained a successful publishing business, producing books on celebrity lifestyles, trades and hobbies and tourist attractions. One of my favorite publications was a bimonthly tabloid in which I not only kept the locals updated on current events and politics but also attracted a popular following from the influx of tourists with legends and strangeness of the Superstition Mountains.

I loved trekking into the mountains and visiting with some of the old prospectors living and working their claims. This, of course, was done with a little danger, due to these prospectors' distrust of outsiders who got too close to their claims. On more than one occasion, I heard a warning shot whiz by my head. There have been several reporters and treasure hunters who have gone into the mountains never to be seen again, but those stories will be set aside for another time in another book.

Another tight-lipped group whose members liked holding their cards close to their chests was the Native American Indians living both on and off the reservations. If you are lucky, you may gain their trust, and if you do, they may share some very interesting stories on the mysteries of the mountain. I recall one time when I wanted to write a series in my publication the *Tattler* about the plight of the Apache Indians. After going through the proper channels, a group of about five elders came into my office and sat around for two days, not talking to me, just observing me and the people I associated with. After receiving their approval, a meeting was arranged with an elderly woman whom they referred to as Grandmother. Her stories started out slow, but the more confident she became with me, the more she shared. She shared with me not only the plight of the Apache but also the spirits of the mountains, sacred rituals, tunnels systems within the mountains, the sky people and even some of the spirits and people that live within the invisible realms and inner earth. Of course, some of this was told to me in strictest confidence, and to this very day, I have honored her request to keep to myself that which is hidden.

Coming out of the mountains for supplies, a few of the old prospectors would stop in at my office in Apache Junction and tell me their stories of strange encounters in the mountains and their search for the elusive treasures of the Peralta Gold and the Lost Dutchman.

I fondly remember this one colorful character who gifted me with a glass quart jar filled with moonshine that he proudly boasted of having made himself. While I could not get past the smell of the 'shine, the old prospector had no problem sipping away on it as he settled into one of my office chairs to share some of his stories about the Superstition Mountains. The man's skin was darkened by the harsh Arizona sun, and he had a large nose that tipped upward at the end. In his dusty weather-worn and stained hat and boots that came midway up his legs, he looked so much like an oversized leprechaun, I couldn't help but wonder if perhaps he was one.

But whether he had been just one of the many colorful human mountain characters or an illusion created by a trickster, I still found the weaving of his storytelling captivating. He inspired me into taking another look at the legends of the mountains, especially his stories about a race of Little People who moved inside the mountain for protection from a race of Giants who had taken over their lands. I even found myself doing a little Dutchman hunting out in the mountains with my boys, Tom and Bob. Although we never found any of the Dutchman's gold, we sure did create some incredible memories, which was worth more to me than all the treasures ever found in the Sups!

As far as ghosts were concerned, I never had much interest in them until years later, when Brad and I moved back to Wisconsin to what we thought was a rather quiet midwestern town called Burlington. But how could I not take interest in ghosts when, without realizing it, we had just moved into one of the most haunted towns in the nation!

My journey into the paranormal began when we moved into this adorable one-bedroom cottage right off Brown's Lake. It was shaded with large elm trees, and the property ran right up to the lake with its own private dock. Its solitude was the perfect environment for me to complete a book I was writing, *Living in the Light, Believe in the Magic*. The peace and solitude I felt there, however, didn't last long. In less than a month of living in our new home, strange things began to happen.

I remember one evening, we were watching television when Brad began to fidget and grunt with annoyance. Realizing that there was nothing on the show that could have caused his agitation, I asked him what was wrong. To my amazement, he explained that a family of ghosts had walked past the television and blocked his view. Although, I was watching the show with him and hadn't seen anything, I was still curious as to what he saw. He described them to me as etheric yet having form. They reminded him of waves one sees coming off the hot pavement in the heat of summer. Knowing my husband does not give way to imagination, I accepted his account and mentally filed it away as an interesting ghost story to someday share with my friends. It was only later that I realized a good ghost story can be fun and even exciting until it becomes personal.

One morning, the innocent hauntings of what Brad later came to call his friends gave way to another type of haunting by something far more dark and sinister, and I was its victim! Brad had left for work, and I awakened from my sleep to the sun coming through my bedroom window and the sound of singing birds. Just as I was having a good stretch, the light of my bedroom turned dark, and the entire room filled with dark emotions of abomination. I felt this invisible presence rush over to the bed where I lay. In an instant, I could feel its attack on me, pushing me down on my back. I could feel its heat, its anger and its desire to hurt me—or even worse.

Out of pure fear, I went into survival mode. Since I couldn't flee from this unknown presence, I took the only alternative left—I attacked back! I returned anger with anger and demanded for it to get out of my house and never come back. When I felt it pull back, I jumped out of my bed and repeated my command and called upon Christ to protect me and drive him out of the house. To my utter relief, it worked. The darkness dissipated, the light came back into the room, the void was replaced with the sound of birds chirping and a sense of peace once again filled the room. After this, I never again felt safe in the house on Brown's Lake.

A short time after this event, we had the opportunity to lease a two-story building on North Pine Street in Burlington's historical district. There we opened an antique and collectible shop in the lower level and moved into the upstairs apartment. It was only after we leased this building that we learned that the entire historical district of Burlington was built over twenty-seven ancient burial mounds, and just like in the movie *Poltergeist*, they did not move the bodies. These spirits were restless! Upon further investigation, digging through the local library newspaper archives, I found an article written by the *Burlington Standard Press*. The article stated that upon digging the foundation of the building we were living in, construction workers found the skeletal remains of a woman and small child. The stage was set for paranormal activity, and activity there was.

With Brad and my two sons, Tom and Bob, on the road building homes, I kept myself busy during the day working at our store and in the evenings working on my websites, my book and my internet radio show, BUFO Radio.

During the daylight hours, things seemed to be pretty normal, but as darkness fell, the paranormal activity rose. This was not isolated to just our apartment, but my neighbor Trudy was also experiencing some pretty strange activities in her apartment. Just for the sake of our own sanity, we concocted a plan that if things got too spooky, one of us would knock on the wall, and the other would rush over.

One night as I was working on my computer, something turned off all the lights in the house, including the television. Then the television was turned back on, showing a black screen with the words "hello….hello…hello" running on the screen over and over again. I was so frightened I forgot about our plan and ran out of the upstairs apartment, down the stairs and stood in the middle of the street, in hopes that a police officer would drive by. Fortunately for me, one never did.

In my mind, I have often replayed the scenario whereby the police officer did appear. I have asked myself the questions "What would have gone through the officer's mind as he came upon the scene of a frightened middle-aged woman in her pajamas standing in the middle of Main Street? How would he have reacted to my pleading with him to go upstairs and check out my apartment for ghosts?"

One evening, I was interviewing Chris Moon, the publisher of a magazine that focused on the paranormal. During the interview, I broke down and told him about the paranormal activities going on in my apartment.

He offered to do a full investigation of my place but requested that I do an initial investigation prior to him and his crew coming out. I confessed that I had not the slightest idea on how to go about investigating ghosts.

Understanding my situation, Chris suggested that I purchase both a digital camera and a tape recorder and instructed me on how to use these as tools for documenting paranormal activity. He went on to say if I got any evidence, he and his crew would follow up.

Per his instructions, I purchased the required equipment and set off to do my first investigation. I will never forget how shocked I was to see strange balls of light and wisps of what looked like smoke on my photographs! I was later to learn that these were orbs and ectoplasms.

This initial investigation opened my eyes to the realization that we are not alone. We share this space with other worlds and beings that are very real yet completely invisible to our spectrum of vision.

I contacted Chris Moon and told him he need not come to Burlington and that I would be conducting my own investigation. Having been an investigative reporter in Arizona, I knew all too well that a good investigation takes leg work and a lot of door knocking. As I interviewed my neighbors, I recognized a pattern developing, a pattern that many might not want to concede to or want divulged. Starting in a small circle working outward, I asked my neighbors if any of them had had any ghostly or paranormal encounters. To my surprise they all said yes. Although I found their answers unsettling, they were also somewhat comforting in that I then knew I was not the only one seeing things.

Expanding my search past the immediate area, I was flabbergasted to hear that everyone in the Burlington area had a personal story to tell of a haunting. Realizing this, the question stood out like an elephant in the room: Why was Burlington experiencing such a wide array of paranormal activity?

It was only later that I learned Burlington and its surrounding area lie right smack in the middle of a strong vortex, which I gave the name the Burlington Vortex.

Science explains that the Earth is powered by a life force that emits electromagnetic energies. The Native American Indians believe that the earth is female, a live breathing entity of which we are all part. Her blood is the energy that runs through her veins, known in the metaphysical world as ley lines. As a rule, ley lines don't usually cross over one another, but if they do, the cross section is called a nexus point. At this intersection, rifts are formed that cause tears in the fabric of reality as we know it. Paranormal spots are caused by these rifts. Burlington lies on one of these points, which affects not only the area but also the people living in it.

Frequency of rift openings is determined by the relative strength of the nexus point. If a strong nexus exists, the chance to split reality occurs more frequently. Our ancient ancestors understood the importance of these hot spots and marked them with earthen mounds, temples, pyramids and large manitou (spirit) stones. Understanding this, I use these clues in my search for the paranormal, knowing that wherever I find these ancient markers I will certainly find anomalies, whether they are cryptids, angels, ghosts, fairies, UFOs, alternate realities, time lines and/or strange creatures that nightmares are made of.

PART I
HAUNTED BURLINGTON

CHAPTER 1
HAUNTED CEMETERIES

The earliest earthen and rock mounds were built by a race of people we know today as the Mound Builders. According to Celtic mythology, the ancient mounds or *sidhe* (pronounced "she") were portals to the other worlds, accessed by astral flight. The Mound Builders placed monoliths, dolmens and henges (gateways) at locations that form interlocking grids. The Native American Indians revered these areas as holy ground and left the land alone for the spirits of their ancestors to roam. The first Europeans, however, used the sacredness of the land to build churches and cemeteries on. Even today, you find many of the cemeteries built on hills, which in most cases are earthen mounds marking portals into the other worlds. And for this reason, these cemeteries have more than the average number of ghostly sightings, which is the case for some of Burlington's most haunted cemeteries.

POTTER'S FIELD

An antiquated little cemetery known in the ghost-hunting community as Potter's Field is considered to be one of the oldest and most haunted cemeteries in Burlington. It was built on an earthen mound behind the newer cemetery, off Highway W.

Not knowing the name of the cemetery at the time and based on the unkempt condition I found it in, I gave it the name Potter's Field, much

This page and opposite: These tombstones were photographed in Potter's Field Cemetery, located off Highway W outside Burlington. This cemetery was built on an ancient burial mound and is considered by the locals to be the most haunted. Hellhounds and some entities with red eyes have been reported seen there.

to the awkwardness of some of the local citizens of Burlington who had ancestors buried there, including some of the founding fathers of the town. I later tried changing it to Mound Cemetery off Highway W, but its popularity had caught on to such an extent that the name Potter's Field stuck.

Due to this new popularity, the cemetery committee eventually cleaned it up, moving the broken tombstones and cutting back the brush that had overtaken a portion of it. Unfortunately, by removing the broken tombstones, visitors do not know where the original burials lie and unknowingly walk on the graves, which I can only imagine disrupts the peace of the spirits that have made this little cemetery their home.

The area it was built on is populated with a series of ancient mounds, located off Brown's Lake. Prior to its present name, Brown's Lake was known to the Native American Indians of that area as Lake of the Shining Arrow. Since there have been numerous reports of UFOs sighted around and over the lake, I assume that the name Shining Arrow was a reference to UFOs. Many of the UFO researchers believe that the UFOs use the portals for multidimensional travel, moving from one dimensional world to another, as do ghosts.

Serious paranormal researchers as well as paranormal thrill seekers have reported to me their startling stories. One of the more common stories is about the feelings of being watched by something that they cannot see. Others have reported being chased out of the cemetery by something with red eyes. Others have reported seeing a hell hound, describing a large black dog with red eyes that has the ability to appear and disappear. In our investigation of the cemetery, we have photographed a mist coming out of a grave and full apparitions standing next to their tombstones.

ST. MARY'S CEMETERY

Another favorite place for the ghost hunters is St. Mary's Cemetery, which is also built on an earthen mound, located right in Burlington off Highway 36, not far from St. Mary's Church.

A mother, daughter and friend went out to the cemetery one evening and described seeing what they thought to be a soldier. The daughter described it as a partial sighting with only the lower half of his body manifesting next to a tombstone. After seeing this apparition, the women decided they had enough of ghost hunting for the evening!

The charred windows of the old Bell Tower at St. Mary's Church still bear witness to the unexplained beam of light and the fire that occurred days after the event.

Strange lights have also been reported seen floating around the cemetery grounds.

We had a report come into our office about a deer ghost but later found out that it was an albino deer that was merely taking a short cut through the cemetery. White deer are quite commonly seen and photographed in the Burlington area. The Native American Indians believe them to be "guardians" of the area.

St. Mary's Church has an interesting story that deserves its spot in the pages of strangeness. In the 1970s, a beam of light came down from the heavens and lit up the church steeple for two days. To this day, no one knows what the beam of light was or why it shone on the steeple. Several days after the beam of light ceased, a mysterious fire broke out in the church's bell tower. The fire report blamed the incident on what was termed "cold lightning." Charred remains and smoke-stained windows still bear witness to the mysterious fire.

Reports have also come into our office about the church having a large underground tunnel system that runs under the church and links to some of the surrounding houses. Today, people living in these houses have heard strange voices, thinking them to be ghosts. Sometimes, I just wonder if these ghostly voices are in fact someone or something still using the tunnel systems to move about unknown and unseen by the community.

One of the local historians in Rochester related to several of our researchers that the town folk sealed their tunnel entrances years ago. According to him, the town's people were hearing eerie cries, howls and screams coming from the tunnels. Due to religious superstition, the people believed the screams were demonic sounds coming from hell and mutually agreed that the entrances should be sealed forever more. Out of fear, no one ventured into the tunnels to find the true source of the strange sounds.

DEADMAN'S HILL CEMETERY

Located off Spring Prairie Road near the railroad tracks is an old 1800s cemetery that sits atop an ancient earthen mound or tumuli. Unseen and forgotten by most of the Burlington locals, the passerby would, in most likelihood, assume this mound to be just a small hill. At the top of the mound, the visitor will find gnarled and twisted trees, formed from growing in a very strong spinning vortex.

Today, little is left of the cemetery, but you can still find some of the tombstones, which have been knocked down and broken by grazing cattle. Looking closely, you can see indentations in the ground caused by the earth settling on graves from an even older burial site, where a great battle took place between the Native American Indians and a Caucasian race of red-

This twisted and gnarled tree evidences the strong twisting vortex atop Deadman's Hill.

The gnarled and twisted trees found on Deadman's Hill, overlooking Honey Creek, mark the site of an ancient battlefield. It is on this vortex site that we found a time portal. Both the Bray Road Beast (Wisconsin werewolf) and Bigfoot have been sighted in this area. The Beast was seen by a neighbor boy when he was coming off the hill carrying two dead sheep.

haired giants, known to the Indians as the Hu-Kadesh or Hu-Kodesh. (See my book *The Red-Haired Giants: Atlantis in North America* for more information on North American Giants.) The fallen dead were buried where they fell, and the memory of them and their great battle was lost to time.

The Wisconsin werewolf, known as the Bray Road Beast, has been seen on this mound site. Sightings of the Beast described it to be some type of hairy humanoid that walks upright with the head of a dog or wolf.

According to the report given to me, in the '70s, the son of a local farmer spotted some sheep lying dead along the hillside just below the cemetery area. As he went closer to the area, he spotted the beast walking down the hillside carrying dead sheep under each arm. According to my informant, shortly after this incident, the farmer replaced his sheep with cattle.

Based off reports coming into my office about both Bray Road Beast and Bigfoot sightings in that area, I decided that this would be an ideal location to search for dimensional doorways. According to cryptid researcher Linda S. Godfrey, author of *Wisconsin Monsters and Real Wolfmen: True Encounters in Modern America*, these types of creatures may be using the portals to move freely about, going in and out of the multidimensional worlds as they desire.

All that remains of the old cemetery on Deadman's Hill are tombstones broken down by grazing cattle.

This ancient altar stone is found on Deadman's Hill and is believed to have been used for sacrificial ceremonies.

At the top of the mound pointing toward Honey Creek, we found an ancient altar stone. This, we believe, is what the Native American Indians call a manitou (spirit) stone. Photographing the stone, we have noticed it emits a bluish glow. We have also noticed that if someone is photographed touching the stone, a bluish glow seems to start emitting from his or her body.

In his book, *Manitou Stones in Wisconsin*, Herman E. Bender of the Mid-America Geographic Foundation, Inc., states: "The stones together with their physical setting were considered sacred. A certain quality remains as they still retain the power vested in them."

In earlier years, these stones were quite common in North America. Most were later destroyed by the early missionaries while they were converting the traditional beliefs of the indigenous people into Christianity. Some were so large that instead of being destroyed, they were intentionally tipped over in an attempt to disguise their use. Many were destroyed through agricultural land clearing. Up until as late as the 1880s, the few manitou stones still left were found with gifts or offerings from those who were still trying to hold onto the old traditions.

If you encounter a rock that seems to speak to you, consider the spirit, or manitou, that lives within and give some sort of offering. I use tobacco or candy, but anything will do. Even a strand of your hair is considered a good offering. It's the intent of the gift, not the gift itself, that matters.

As we stood at the top of the hill, we all sensed the powerful vortex we were in. There were also signs of the vortex, such as the trees' being twisted and gnarled from the years of growing in the spinning vortex energies. We also found nut trees, which, for reasons unknown to me, grow in these vortex areas.

Not only did we feel the sensations of the vortex, but we actually stepped into a parallel universe! This dimension was so similar to ours that we would have never known about it if one of my friends, Patty, hadn't been watching the time. Fortunately, I had a radio show to do at 8:00 that evening, and Patty was keeping track of time for me so that I wouldn't be late getting back to the station.

At one point, she looked at her cellphone, exclaiming that we had to leave since it was already 7:33 p.m. and I would be late for my own show! Hearing this, we headed down off the hill and back to the car. The distance wasn't far, and it only took us two to three minutes to complete the journey back. After we arrived at the car, one of the girls, Sharon, announced that Patty was off on her time. Sharon said that according to her clock on the dash board of the car, the time was only 7:18. This was a fifteen minute time difference. While the girls were arguing over the time difference, I had Brad check the time on his watch. His watch also read 7:18. Well Patty grabbed her cell phone to take one more look. To her and all of our amazement, her cellphone time now read the same as Sharon and Brad's time—7:18! Patty's phone had change back from 7:33 to 7:18! How strange is that? Well, you are about to find out.

Fortunately, I was interviewing Dr. Clifford Alford on my radio show that evening. Dr. Alford is very familiar with space/time distortion and portals. I related the story to Clifford about our time experience at Dead Man's Hill. He explained that we had stepped into a parallel world or alternate reality while on the hill, a dimension almost exact to ours—except it existed fifteen minutes into our future. He then went on to tell me that while we were in the other world, we should have noticed distortions or seen, through our peripheral vision, things moving about. After he said this, I recalled Sharon making comments to all of us about seeing just this type of phenomena. He also said, we were lucky that we came out the same way as we went in, or we could have been stuck in that world permanently. After listening to Clifford, I now make sure to exit a portal area the same way I went in. We were lucky that day. We found the portal, we entered and we experienced its uniqueness. Fortunately for us, we safely exited the same way as we went in and can now bear witness that such places do exist! (I have taken several people to this location, and each time, my watch showed the same anomaly I experienced with Brad and the girls, thus showing this area as having a permanent portal into another dimension in time.)

CHAPTER 2
BIGFOOT ENCOUNTERS

Another creature that has been reported to use the portals and hide within the dimensional veil is the Bigfoot. In the '70s, a Bigfoot was sighted near Deadman's Hill, in a swampy and wooded area near the railroad tracks. One of the hunters who was there that night gave me the report of their encounter. Because he does not want his name released, I will simply call him Bruce.

According to his story, several men from Chicago had joined up with him and a few of their friends from Burlington to do some hunting. They had all brought their gear to set up camp for a few days and nights out by Deadman's Hill. They chose their campsite in a somewhat remote area surrounded by woods and swamps with the railroad tracks and Honey Creek running behind.

That evening, while sitting around the campfire, they began hearing yelps, howls and loud screams coming from the area of where the old Burlington Egg Plant is located, which coincidentally is adjacent to what we call the Haunted Woods, off Honey Creek Road.

They could hear the yelps from the dogs as they chased something large that was heading in their direction. Periodically, they would hear the pursued creature give out a loud and inhuman scream as it blindly ran into barbed-wire fencing.

The men in the hunting group were standing up with their guns, listening to the sounds. Whatever this thing was, it was heading straight for their camp! Soon, through the light of their campfire and a nearly full moon, they saw a humanoid-type hairy creature about eight feet tall, dark in color and running upright. Bruce said that it ran past their campsite and made its way across the railroad, crossing Honey Creek and disappearing into the woods on the opposite shore.

The next day, the hunters walked around looking for tracks and any other evidence they could find of what they knew to be a Bigfoot. Bruce claims they found large footprints in the soft ground and mud around the swamp, and where the creature had run into the barbed wire, they found pieces of hair. The hair was allegedly taken back to Chicago by his friends.

While some Bigfoot researchers believe that these humanoids are a physical creature, there are others that believe that they may be skin walkers or shape shifters that can take on a physical shape.

Native American shamans tell us that our human evolutionary tree is much bigger than we think and has hidden branches that, as of yet, we cannot perceive. They describe these hidden branches of the human evolutionary tree as being very similar to us, characterizing them as neither absolute good nor absolute evil. They explain them to have the same type of

These humanoids still walk the woods of Burlington. We photographed this Bigfoot print in 2011 in the woods not far from the sighting of the hunters.

fears and emotions as we do. They avoid human contact by camouflaging themselves, much like the chameleon. They can also cloak themselves by creating a cloud of invisibility, or they can escape through the portals leading into other multidimensional worlds and realities.

Joan Ocean, a cetacean researcher famous for her underwater dolphin communication project, has the following to say about the Bigfoot:

> *On many occasions we have noticed that our Sasquatch friends appear see-through, and seemingly vanish instantaneously. The Ancient Ones can dematerialize. They are able to move freely between our three-dimensional, linear reality, and their world, which exists outside our conventional laws of physics, in the expanded world of Quantum Physics. In the physical world we know, they make shelters, forage for food, walk long distances, eat, sleep, defecate, communicate and make loud growling sounds. In their extra-dimensional world, life is different. Their bodies are of a different frequency and therefore their needs are not the same as when in a three-dimensional, physical environment. The particular group of Wise Ones that I have been introduced to can only remain out of body for limited periods of time, or they lose their ability to return to physical matter.*
>
> *There are many other advanced beings that can access the refined frequencies of light in lighter bodies as well. The Ancient Ones have told me they are in contact with the Good Star People, who also know how to live in nearby, and very accessible, parallel realities. Physicists know that in Quantum Physics electrons can pass through solid matter. Similarly, while in a quantum state, the Wise Ones have no weight or mass; they are like a "wave" of energy, or perhaps like an Orb.*

The question has always been how can these creatures exist without more people seeing and reporting them? To this I answer, based on personal observation, that they have the ability to create and hide in what I refer to as a cloud of invisibility.

I came to understand how these entities cloaked themselves while researching a UFO flap in Burlington. For almost one year, the UFOs were appearing nightly over Burlington. Several times, while trying to photograph and document these nightly visitations, I would feel a presence standing next to me. Refusing to believe that it was only my imagination, I began photographing the spots where I felt the presence. I was semi-successful with this process, yet most times, the photo would only show some sort of an undistinguishable shadowy form standing inside what looked like a large greenish/yellow cloud. One evening, however, I got lucky when the alien I was trying to photograph dropped his guard, and I was able to capture a more distinguishable image of him standing inside the veil. This brought me to the realization that we are being observed by various entities that have the ability to hide themselves within a cloud of invisibility. I believe that they use their mind abilities to pull in and surround themselves with vital life force known as the *prana* or *chi*. They then create a vortex by spinning the electrons at a speed beyond our spectrum of vision so that anything standing within the vortex would be invisible to any observer.

To prove that this could be done, I created a means for myself and others to accumulate this same type of *prana* with our minds and pull it down to us. As of yet, I have not figured out how to intentionally manipulate the field where we can stand inside and become invisible to the observer. I have, however, been able to pull the *prana* to us and use it to separate the ethereal self from the physical self for the purpose of dimensional travel.

My theory on hiding within a cloud of invisibility may not be such a stretch as you may think, and it is certainly nothing new. Actually, the

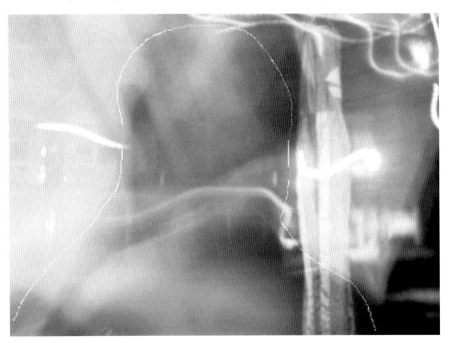

An alien stands within a cloud of invisibility; the cloud usually appears as yellow-green in color.

Opposite, top: Mary Sutherland demonstrates how to pull in *prana* to a young man.

Opposite, bottom: Mary Sutherland not only has the ability to teach her students how to separate the ethereal self from the physical self for dimensional travel but also, as you see, has the capability to photograph the event as it takes place.

Above: Using a digital camera, Mary Sutherland photographs the ethereal body leaving the physical body for the purpose of dimensional travel.

Left: A spinning vortex. Note that outside the vortex, the photo is clear, but the closer people are to center, the more distorted they become as the vortex spins their molecular bodies from one reality into another dimension.

cloud of invisibility is an old trick and is still used today by shamans. Some of the tribes of the Native American Indians also use this practice in their initiations of manhood. As it was told to me, in order to pass the initiation into manhood, the young man must be able to make himself invisible then walk up to another person and wave his arms in front of him without being seen.

As I understand the practice, it is metaphysically done by pulling out of the ethereal world what we know as *prana* or *chi*, which is composed of electrons. By pulling these electrons together tight enough, a wall is created that allows no light to penetrate through. By standing behind this wall, or within, one becomes invisible to the observer. It would be similar to you putting your hand in between your eyes and the sun. Your hand creates a wall obstructing your vision of the sun. The sun is still there but just not visible for you to see.

BIGFOOT ENCOUNTERS AROUND RAILROAD TRACKS

The story you read about the hunters and Bigfoot near the railroad tracks is not an isolated case. Over ten years ago, a nurse came to my office to report a Bigfoot sighting near Kansasville, which is only a few miles east of Burlington, near Bong Recreational Park. She reported that while driving home one early morning after working the night shift, she had to brake for a Bigfoot crossing the road in front of her. She hesitated before finishing the rest of the story, feeling that if this sighting wasn't strange enough, surely what she was about to tell me would sound almost unbelievable. And in most cases she may have been right, but she had come to the right person for her story. She continued with her story by hesitantly telling me she saw this Bigfoot carrying a construction sign with an attached yellow blinking light under his arm. Even though she was embarrassed to tell me this detail, I found this strange account completely credible. These creatures are very curious, and the flashing light would have certainly attracted the attention of the Bigfoot. I reasoned that it took the sign as a piece of curiosity that it could later inspect or play with. The nurse, who wishes to remain anonymous, told me she watched the Bigfoot cross the road, go through a small patch of open space, cross some railroad tracks and enter into a wooded area.

Years later, I heard of two other Bigfoot sightings on the north side of Burlington in the Honey Creek area. Interestingly enough, both of these sightings took place near the same railroad tracks, twelve to fifteen miles from the nurse's sighting. Being that the tracks run through isolated areas, unseen by most except for maybe a hiker or a hunter, this type of area would be ideal for these creatures to easily travel from one location to another without the concern of being seen.

THE ROCK-THROWING BIGFOOT

Before we get off the subject of Bigfoot, I have another personal story I would like to share about our encounter of Bigfoot in the woods north of Burlington.

The roots of this story take us back to my mother and a restaurant she had in Wisconsin. As a child, I used to observe her giving odd jobs to some of the local school kids to work off what was usually a burger and fries that they could not have afforded otherwise. Some of the older teenage boys loved this arrangement, as they were usually broke and quite hungry after school. It worked so well for her that now as an adult and having a restaurant of my own, I sometimes follow her idea and hire on one of the less fortunate teenage boys, giving them a sense of responsibility and a little cash in their pockets. In most cases, this seems to work quite well for me and the kids I am trying to help—except for one we came to know as "Monkey," who was introduced to me by a self-proclaimed counselor from the local teen outreach center.

Monkey had worked for the café for several months and seemed to have adjusted quite well into the world of employment. I was quite open to allowing his friends to hang out while he worked. Like Monkey, his friends seemed quite genial and caused no problems for the café or with any of the customers that frequented our establishment until one fateful Saturday night.

Unknown to me, Monkey had decided that he and his friends could do much better for themselves if they created their own online business. Since they didn't have money to purchase inventory to sell, they had devised an elaborate scheme to rob our store and use the stolen merchandise to establish their business. The plan was that Monkey would tag along with me on my Saturday Night Haunted Tours into the woods of Burlington. While he was with me, he would keep in contact with his friends on his cellphone as they robbed the café.

He called them when we arrived at the woods, which was their go ahead to kick in the basement door that led to a trapdoor that opens into the café upstairs. In the darkness and out of sight from any surveillance cameras, they would then be free and undisturbed for several hours to clean out my merchandise and vandalize the store. Since Monkey was constantly on the phone talking to one friend or another, I suspected nothing and took our tour group out into the woods to what we call the "Sacred Circle." It was at the circle that all hell broke loose.

The usual routine is when we arrive, I sit the group down on these large rocks under some cedar trees, tell them stories of the woods' strangeness and photograph them. We usually stay there for several hours, allowing the group ample time to photograph orbs, run EVP sessions and experience whatever the woods has to offer that night as far as the paranormal goes. As we began to sit down, Monkey left the group and walked over to a shadowy area to make a phone call to his friends, apparently to make sure they got in OK and to give them further instructions on what to do next. While he may have been out of earshot from the group, he was not out of earshot from a group of Bigfoot that was standing in the shadows behind the trees where he stood, and they did not like what they were hearing.

To get my attention of the danger that I and the store were in, a family of Bigfoot started tossing small stones into the group. Being that rock throwing from Bigfoot is not an unusual thing for us to experience in these woods, most just acknowledged their presence and went on talking among themselves. A few tried photographing in the direction the stones seemed to have been thrown from. As Monkey joined the group, the rock throwing dramatically increased, and the Bigfoot began throwing larger stones. Fearing that someone might get hurt but not wanting to leave, I had the group pick up their gear and move to another place farther away from the circle. I thought that maybe the Bigfoot, for some reason, did not want us sitting on those stones and that by moving we would be safe. I was quite wrong because the Bigfoot started pelting us with stones from every direction. By now it was quite obvious to me and the group that we were under attack. In my mind, I was asking myself why this was happening. We had always been welcomed by them. What in the world had set them off like this?

The people in the group, including myself, were quite frightened over this violent encounter and decided to shut the tour down and get out of the woods as quickly as possible! Because it was dark and we had only a few flashlights to light our way over a rocky trail, we could not move as fast as we wanted to. The whole time we were trying to get out of the woods as quickly and safely as possible, we were ducking stones of all sizes being tossed at us from various directions. As I was outwardly trying to keep the group as calm as possible, inwardly I was praying that none of the rocks would hit us in the head and severely hurt us. It seemed that as long as we maintained a fast walk, the rock tossing would slow down, but as soon as we began to slow, the rocks would start coming at a much faster pace, as if they were herding us like sheep or cattle. After we exited the first sector of woods, I told the group we should be safe since, in all my encounters with the Bigfoot, they never seemed to throw stones except in the first woods from where we escaped. As the group stopped to catch their breath and grab some sense of comfort, a very large stone came whizzing past my head, hitting a utility pole that I was standing next to. The stone was about the size of a soccer ball and hit the pole so hard it caused the pole to vibrate, leaving a small indentation in the wooden pole. I could not help but think that if that stone would have hit my head it would have popped it like a melon. Fortunately for us, the group of Bigfoot had good aim with no intention of hitting me with the stone. However, I honestly did not think that at the time.

We were so frightened most of us were in tears. Tina Caskey, who was helping me that night with the tour, had a severe asthma attack just as we started back onto the trail leading into the second woods. This was the last woods we needed to go through before we could get to the parking lot and the safety of our cars. To make matters worse, as Tina experienced her asthma attack, she realized that she had not brought her inhaler. Things had just gone from worse to critical. Tina could not pull any oxygen into her lungs and was struggling. There was no way that she could walk or save herself from the continued attack. It was crucial that she stop and calm down. Realizing this, I stood next to Tina and began yelling at the Bigfoot to knock it off! I breathlessly explained to them that Tina was seriously ill and needed to calm down or she could die. As if they understood what I was telling them, the rock throwing instantly stopped and the woods became very still. I worked with Tina on her breathing until she stabilized and gave the OK to continue the walk out of the woods. And just as soon as she said she was better, the rock throwing started back up again, not quite as violently. They continued herding us out of the woods with the rock throwing until we got into the parking lot where our cars were. It was only then that the attack ceased.

Since we were all shaken from the attack, all anyone wanted to do was get in their cars and go back to the café, where we could calm down and try to understand what had just happened.

Still in shock over our encounter, we arrived back at the café. It was there that I finally understood why the family of Bigfoot was so insistent for us to leave the woods.

What I had thought was a violent attack by the Bigfoot was not that at all. I will always believe that they overheard Monkey talking to his friends and realized that our place was in the process of being robbed while we were in the woods. In their own way, they were trying to rescue me and save the café.

After arriving at the parking lot, Monkey made his final call alerting his friends to our unexpected early return. Because of this family of Bigfoot, the robbery was kept at a minimal amount of damage to the store, and Monkey's newly formed little gang was not able to clean me out of all my inventory, except for what I had out on display.

The Burlington Police Department was on the ball and immediately went into action to recover what had been stolen, and several arrests were later made. Fortunately, I had insurance, which covered my damages and replaced articles that were not recovered. I never did tell the police what had taken place with the Bigfoot that night nor the real reason why we called off the tour and came back early. I felt it may have been just a little bit "too paranormal" for them to include in their report.

We went back to the woods the following Saturday and experienced no rock throwing. It has been several years since this time, and the Bigfoot have never repeated this type of action.

CHAPTER 3

THE WHITE BEAST
OF BOHNERS LAKE

Following is a Bigfoot case witnessed and written by our friend and fellow researcher Tina Caskey. We call the case the "White Beast of Burlington."

I live in a small lake area called Bohners Lake, just northwest of Burlington, Wisconsin. At the time of this tale, I lived on the opposite side of the lake from where I live now, about a half mile away from a Boy Scout camp called Camp Oh-Da-Ko-Ta. This camp, located off Dyer Lake, is made up of 185 acres of beautiful rolling hills and woodlands.

It was a beautiful summer day, so I decided to take a walk with my dogs, a golden retriever and an English setter. I went a different way than usual and happened upon the back trail to the camp. It was chained off, but I chanced it anyway and hopped over to check it out.

The trail was very quiet and peaceful, and we walked a while enjoying ourselves greatly. After a bit, we came to some buildings. One was a large pole barn type that had its doors chained shut. Curiosity overtook me, as usual, and I went up and pushed on one of the large doors, allowing a crack of about six inches. I tried peering inside and couldn't see much but a floor and empty space.

I was shocked when an earsplitting roar came out of the barn. It sounded like a scream but had a deep, guttural and bearlike sound.

Upon hearing this, my dogs took off running, and I, being terrified, took off running after them. We ran back to my house, and shaking like a leaf and out of breath, I told my (now ex-) husband what had happened. He, of course, told me that what I had heard was merely a crane. Hearing his explanation, I just stared at him incredulously. Knowing better, I decided to not argue the point with him. I would just ponder on this by myself and try to calm down.

The day went on and nothing else was said about it until just after dark, when we both heard the same scream coming from the backyard.

The house I lived in at the time had a huge backyard. At the very back, we had a garden by a small wooded area, and it was from there that we heard the scream. Well, my ex grabbed his rifle and the dogs, and headed down to the garden, finding nothing.

He came back to the house, his eyes wide, and acknowledged that what I had heard was not a crane.

After that, we went about our night talking about it, with the dogs nervously prancing about. We eventually went to bed.

Being summer, I left the bedroom windows open for some breeze. About 3:00 a.m., I was jolted out of my sleep. The beast had presented itself right outside my bedroom window with a loud bone chilling scream. The dogs were so frightened they never barked. I found them cowering next to each other for comfort or protection, whining.

My husband jumped out of the bed and grabbed his rifle. He had to go outside alone to investigate without the dogs, as they didn't want to have anything to do with it, but just as before, he found nothing.

Well the story would end here, as we didn't hear anything after that and I was too scared to investigate the building again, but three weeks later, the beast returned. My husband and I went away for the weekend on a camping trip, leaving my mother, younger sister and her two daughters to housesit and take care of our dogs until our return.

The following morning, my sister was in the kitchen cooking breakfast when my niece Sandra came in. She looked at the kitchen window and noticed a long smear mark.

Sandra was about nine at the time and looked up at my sister and said, "I know what did that." My sister looked at it and asked Sandra what she thought made it.

Sandra replied, "Oh, it was the Swamp Monster." My sister chuckled and asked her why she thought that.

Now, I was always teasing the girls with stories about a swamp monster that lived out by me, so they just knew that there was a creature out there.

This, of course, was before my own experience, and now it wasn't cute and funny anymore.

Then she said, "I saw the Swamp Monster last night."

My sister said, chuckling still, "Oh, what did you see?"

Sandra just looked at her and said, "I saw a huge white hairy arm, and it ran its claws across Aunt Tina's bedroom screen." (She was talking about my bedroom.)

My sister asked, "Wow, what did you do?"

Sandra said, "Aw, I just rolled over and went to sleep. I knew it was just Aunt Tina trying to scare me."

Of course, we were camping.

So, what did she see? I haven't a clue to this day. But I wonder, were they keeping something out there, or was there something living in that barn unbeknownst to them at the camp and did it follow me home?

Last summer my brother, sister-in-law and I tried going back there, but we were stopped by the person living across the road.

Before finalizing this report, I would like to add one more detail about this particular camp. Before our encounter, a group of us had gotten together to check out Dyer Lake and do some night swimming. We drove through the front entrance to the camp, which is at the center edge of the lake. We had to be quiet, as this was private property and we had not gotten permission to be there.

Using our flashlights, we tried following the trail but ended up somehow getting off it. We went over a hillside and, there at the bottom of the hill, found a beautiful iron gate about six feet tall. We noticed that there was a hole dug into the side of the hill and this gate was being used to cover the opening.

Opening the gate and crawling through, we found ourselves in a twelve-by twelve-foot cave of sorts. Inside this cave, we found candles, a dead rooster and a scythe. There was nothing else. No altar or other signs of occult practices, just the things we found haphazardly lying about the room. My sister's now ex-husband took the scythe (which I told him to leave there), and we left and never went back—that is, until I went for my walk that summer day and heard the Beast.

⋙◈◈⋘

I have done several tours at Bohners Lake, both daytime and nighttime. I personally do not mind taking people out there during the day, but several times during evening tours, we have had near encounters with something large and humanoid. Because this area is known for cryptid encounters and us never having a good look at it, I cannot determine if this was the same creature Tina and her family encountered or something entirely different.

The place where we have had our encounters with what we thought to be a swamp monster is in a small lagoon that connects the old fish hatchery (off Fish Hatchery Road) to Bohners Lake. Several times while walking a group along the path leading to the lake, we could hear something swimming in lagoon, always in the shadows, so we couldn't get a good look at it. By the sounds of it, the creature had to have been at least 150–200 pounds, and based on the strokes, it was at least five to six feet in height. We could hear the strokes of the creature swimming in the water, stroking with one arm, followed by another stroke of the other arm. As we walked, it would swim with us, adjusting its strokes to our speed. We had the eerie feeling we were being stalked by this aquatic creature. When we stopped, it would stop, and when we started again, it would start. After several times of this creature making its appearance known, I ceased doing any further evening tours at Bohners Lake.

CHAPTER 4

THE HOUSE ON RANDALL STREET

THE PERFECT STORM

As I listened to Jeannie and her children tell me their story about the house on Randall Street, I observed how strong and dynamic their life forces were. I also noted that they were all very open to the idea of life after death and that the deceased could communicate and interact with us through spirit. Combining the energies of Jeannie's family and the comings and goings of various spirits with the manifestation energies of a paranormal hot spot, on which the house was built, a "Perfect Storm" was created.

In nearly two decades of my research on the paranormal, I have found that our attention or focus is concentrated energy that we direct at something. This type of energy is used by all life forms, including spirits, as a food source. As the life form feeds on the fodder provided by your thoughts, it becomes stronger, and in the case of a spirit, manifestation becomes possible.

It is my belief that we are not alone but rather connected to a cosmic consciousness of the "all that is." Everything that has been created, whether it be organic or inorganic—land or mineral, animal, insect, bird or human (coldblooded or warmblooded)—has consciousness. This consciousness is designed as an intelligent energy that we are constantly interacting with whether we are aware of it or not.

Being children of the creator, we inherited the "God gene," a unique gift that separates us from all others. This gift is what ancient texts refer to as the "spark of life." This spark is, in electrical terms, called a charge. When this charge is directed, through attention or focus, we have the capability to bringing life to a dead cell or to activate something that has been inactive for centuries or longer. Opening dimensional doorways, activating dormant vortices, bringing back spirits, healing or bringing about misfortunes or sickness, UFO sightings and cryptid encounters just scratch the surface as to what our focus can manifest.

The more focus the human being gives to an object, whether it be organic, inorganic or spirit, the stronger the life force of that object becomes. After a certain amount of time of continuous feeding on concentrated energy, the object, having its own intelligence and state of consciousness, can separate and live independently from its creator. No longer being dependent on its creator for a food source, it can move about feeding off other energy sources. Ancient texts refer to these independent entities of consciousness as "tulpoids." These entities hunt for their food much like the rest of those in the animal kingdom. Some actively go out stalking their prey while others just quietly lie in wait until the food source comes to them—and then, they pounce.

In Jeannie's case, I found that the land, the house and the entities lie in wait for their prey to take up residency. The combination of their life energies and acceptance of spirits awakened the house and provided the perfect fodder for what lived there. Jeannie knew of several people who had died in the house. In the downstairs back bedroom, a woman by the name of Mary had died of cancer, and a man died in one of the bedrooms upstairs. Although, for privacy's sake, I cannot give the address of the house, I will tell you that the house used to be used as the convent for the nuns of St. Mary's Church. In the basement is a tunnel, now sealed, that runs from the old convent to St. Mary's rectory. They also found a small door nailed shut that opened up to stairways leading to a secret room hidden within the walls of the house. The backyard at one time extended out to where there is now the paved parking lot behind St. Mary's School. It was in this area that what they called the "Black Man" was first spotted. Apparently the Black Man's territory extended to the house because he was also sighted inside. Both of Jeannie's children had seen the Black Man step out of the wall, walk through the room and disappear into another wall. Although the children could see him, he gave no indication that he had sensed their presence. Jeannie and her husband had converted the back bedroom into a playroom. One evening as Jeannie and her husband were in the dining room visiting with some family members from out of state, the kids, who were playing in the playroom, started screaming the "Black Man, the Black Man!" All the children saw the Black Man step out of the wall and walk into a closet. At the very same time this was happening, two-thirds of the people sitting in the dining room heard the very loud ringing of a large church bell. Jeannie explained that it was so loud they were holding their ears. The other third of the people in the dining room did not hear the bell ringing and were looking at those who did with utter astonishment, not realizing what was going on.

Jeannie told me that in the beginning, the spirits of the house seemed domestic and harmless. The spirit of an elderly woman would appear and watch over her as she washed diapers and hung them on the clothesline to dry. When she would be down in the basement, she would see the ghost of the woman partially materialize. Jeannie described only seeing the bottom portion of a long dress with the ghost wearing very small brown shoes.

Another common occurrence was with a radio that would start playing loudly. This event would not be of any significance except for the fact that the radio was not plugged in. Jeannie explained that the family had become accustomed to such activities. With twenty-twenty hindsight, she now looks back to this time and feels that the family was in a state of denial. They were comfortable in their home, and instead of facing what most would have considered abnormal, they chose to accept what was going on as normal. For them, it was quite normal to hear footsteps walking around in the attic or going up and down the stairs. It was quite normal to hear strange chanting on a regular basis.

I found myself strangely unnerved by several stories Jeannie told me about her daughter's encounters. (In writing these accounts, I will refer to Jeannie's daughter as "L.") As I was listening to Jeannie and "L's" accounts, I could feel the hair rise on my arms and a chill go up and down my back. I had to ask myself whether the spirit of the house had been using this little girl as a human portal for spirits and unseen entities from the other worlds to navigate.

Jeannie started her stories out with "L" having what they believed to be an angel that watched over her. Her daughter called him "King" because the angel wore a crown. As a small child, "L" remembers being in her crib, watching the window open and King coming through. She also told me that King liked to stack things and played a lot with her building blocks. Jeannie contributed to this story by telling me that he would also go down into her kitchen, stack things on the floor and organize items in her cabinets and on the counter. "L" recalled another story when she and her family were in a car accident. In this scene, King appeared and protected her from being hurt.

I believe it is safe to say that most of us women as little girls had a toy telephone. I know I did. I even remember its color—pink! Oh, the fun conversations we would have on our toy phones, calling our friends and family, inviting them over for tea or coffee. But in the case of "L," imagination became reality. The spirits were using the phone to communicate with "L." Jeannie told me that one day she was in the playroom with "L," and the phone rang. "L" answered the phone, and it was her grandmother calling, "Hi cutie, how's the weather!" Jeannie went on to tell me that they were not only using the phone but also animating toys that "L" had in her room. One toy in particular went off and kept repeating, "Hi, I am Alfie. Let's play." "L" called for her mom, and Jeannie tried turning it off. But it kept playing. So she turned it over on its back to take the batteries out—and yes, as some of you may have already guessed, the toy had no batteries in it! They had been taken out.

The spirits of the house seemed to have accepted "L," but as time went by, Jeannie found herself pregnant. This new pregnancy seemed to have disrupted the normal spirit patterns of the house. The closer Jeannie got to her due date, the more out of control the spirits became. One in particular was extremely obnoxious. One night, Jeannie couldn't sleep and got out of her bed to hear the obnoxious spirit stomping up the stairs mocking Jeannie by yelling out, "I am pregnant…I am sick…I am tired!" He stomped his way all the way up the stairs to the attic, where he stepped inside and slammed the door. Jeannie laughed as she told me, "After he slammed the door, he never came out for the rest of the night." Then Jeannie got a serious look on her face and told me when she knew it was time to pack up the family and leave the house. Shortly after the baby was born, things dramatically changed. It started with the children waking up with drawings on their bodies made by a magic marker. Strange writings of an unknown origin were found on the ceilings and walls. It finally progressed to their awakening to burning sensations on their bodies. As they would look to see what was causing the burning, they would find small claw marks. This was happening to the entire family, including the newborn baby. Jeannie was having dreams of small children being held captive in the cellar of the house. Jeannie did learn, through one of the previous owners of the house, that slaves were hidden in the underground tunnel and cistern that are found in the basement of the house.

Although Jeannie and her family have been gone from this house for over fifteen years, they are still haunted by their experiences and continue to seek answers. It was through their quest that they found me and shared their story. One evening, years later, they went back to the house on Randall Street and took some photos. In the photos, they saw what appeared to be the spirits of children. After listening to their story, around 10:00 p.m. that evening, I and another investigator, along with Jeannie and her family, drove over to the house on Randall Street. And just as Jeannie had photographed, I, too, got a photo of a young boy standing outside the house under a window.

Whether it was the universe working that night confirming Jeannie's story or just plain luck, I will never know, but we didn't just get the photo of the ghost child; we also observed the family then living in that same house, loading up a trailer in the middle of the night. Jeannie went over and introduced herself to the family as a previous tenant, explaining that they were forced to move because of the house being haunted. To my amazement, instead of looking at us like we were delusional, they answered back: "We know. That is why we are moving. We can't spend another night here!"

CHAPTER 5

CIVIL WAR GHOSTS
ON ACADEMY ROAD

Academy Road runs a few miles north of Burlington into the small town of Rochester. Just before entering Rochester, coming from Burlington, on the right side of the road, one will find the stone remnants of what was once a POW camp that imprisoned Confederate soldiers captured during the Civil War. Across the road from this is a historic two-story house built from local fieldstone. There is no sign to mark its existence, and only a few locals still remember the stories told to them by their descendants. This camp would have been forgotten if it were not for the ghosts of Confederate soldiers wandering about and seen by motorists driving down Academy Road.

An elderly couple who lived in this historic house across from the POW camp told me of a terrifying ghostly encounter they had while living there. As it happens with people who have lived together for years, many times they find themselves more comfortable sleeping in separate bedrooms due to the tossing and turning of the other or his or her extensive and loud snoring. This was the case with this couple. The gentleman told me he awoke one morning to some ghostly presence holding him down in his bed. He tried to move but found himself not only paralyzed but also unable to even scream. He was drenched in fear over the encounter yet unable to protect himself. As this was happening to him, he heard his wife scream from her bedroom. Her scream broke the spell the ghost had over him. He jumped up and ran quickly into her room, finding her experiencing the same ghostly attack as he. As he ran to her bed, the ghost released her. He grabbed his wife and held her as she cried. I am sure that most have heard the medical term sleep paralysis, which usually occurs as the victim awakens, and if it had not been for the fact that the couple had both experienced this phenomenon at the same time and in separate rooms, I would have written it off as such. But due to the corresponding event, I have to conclude that this was indeed an attack by several ghosts. After the couple gave me their report, I never saw them again. I have often thought of this couple and have wondered if this was merely a one-time event, or if they have experienced more events since speaking with me.

CHAPTER 6

A HAUNTING ON MORMON ROAD

ollowing is a report filed by Matt H., a Burlington local who came in to
my office one day to give me several stories on his ghostly encounters.
Here is his story.

I was born and raised in Burlington and brought up Lutheran, attending St.
John's Lutheran School from kindergarten through eighth grade.

My first experience, that I remember, was when I was in either first or
second grade. It could have been a few years later, but I know I was young.
We lived on Voree Court off Mormon Road, which connects Highway 36
and Highway 11. I remember hearing my name being called every so often.
Thinking it was my mom or dad, I would go to them and ask what they
wanted. Many times they'd say that they never called for me and told me I
was just hearing things.

I have one clear memory when I was sitting at the kitchen table doing my
homework. I started hearing my name being called but dismissed it as just
hearing things, being that no one other than me was in the house. I started
hearing what sounded like footsteps coming from the living room into the
kitchen. Then something whispered my name in my ear. That was the last
straw—I jumped out of my chair and darted out the back door. I never
stopped running until I was well up the driveway. When I did stop I looked
back at the house to see a dark shadow figure staring at me through the front
door. I ran to the neighbor's house, where an older woman took me in. After
I had calmed down and was able to tell her my story, she tried to convince
me that what I had experienced was just from my overactive imagination,
but I knew different.

CHAPTER 7

Haunting Continues on North Kendrick Street

M att H. continued by telling me another story of a haunting he had on North Kendrick Street.

For years, I was hesitant to talk about my experiences—that was, until my little brother told me about his. He doesn't remember much of anything from our first house. But the hauntings in our second home on North Kendrick Street we both remember all too well.

When I was ten and my brother was eight, we moved to North Kendrick. We lived there for ten years, over which time a number of unexplained things happened. For now, I will only mention a few.

My bedroom was downstairs, which wasn't anything like a creepy basement but quite homey and comfortable. Just like when I was younger, living on Mormon Road, I began hearing my name being called. This time, though, it was different; it was now happening to my brother as well.

Out of the corner of my eye, I would see shadowy figures moving about. I would feel the atmosphere around me change and a presence in the room.

When no one was home or everyone was in bed sleeping, I would hear strange footsteps walking around upstairs.

Other unaccounted for noises, such as bangs, clinks and tapping, were also occurring.

I noticed that when I would get the feeling of a presence nearby, my dog would start responding to it. Sometimes, he would just become fixated on a certain spot. Yet other times, he would walk up to this unseen entity or even follow it as it walked about the room. This started happening quite often.

One night, just as I was about to drift off to sleep, I was physically pushed down into my mattress. I lay there terrified and unable to move except for my eyes, which were opened wide. Then I felt the pressure lift. It wasn't long before I offered to switch rooms with my brother whose room was upstairs.

Not knowing of my ghostly encounters, he jumped at the chance of having his big brother's room. But almost every night, my little brother would end up back in his old room, crying to me that he was having nightmares. He had his room in the basement for about two months before we switched back.

One night, he broke down and told me his secret with a promise I would not tell anyone. After promising him I would keep his secret, he told that the last night he stayed in my room, while lying in bed awake, he felt a pressure force him down into the mattress. My jaw dropped. I knew then that I wasn't imagining what happening—this thing, was very real!

CHAPTER 8
OCCULT PRACTICES

ALIVE, WELL, FLOURISHING

The greatest responsibility in this world that God has laid upon us is to seek after our dead.
—*Joseph Smith,* Doctrines of Salvation

THE WHITE RIVER: RIVER OF THE DEAD

The two rivers flowing through Burlington were ideal waterways for travel. Gravitational anomalies—created, as I believe, from a strong vortex—caused the current of the Fox River to flow into town and the White River to flow out of town.

It was in the White River that the Strangite Mormons baptized their dead by proxy. As I understand it, a living Strangite Mormon would be put into a trance, allowing the spirit of the deceased to temporarily enter his or her body. While the spirit was in the body, the prophet proceeds with the baptism ceremony. When it is done, the spirit of the deceased is released, and the living vessel resumes life as normal. The baptism location can be seen by standing at the bridge in Burlington and looking toward the south.

In Mormonism, there is a keen interest concerning the afterlife. Even the name Mormon hints to this, being that Mormo is the king of the ghouls, or living dead. This is also reflected in both the temple rituals and the genealogical work each Mormon is expected to engage in order to redeem his or her ancestors. Not only do Mormons seek after their dead, but the dead also seek after them. Wilford Woodruff, the fourth president of the

Above: In Sacred Geometry, the number 11 represents dimensional doorways. All roads going through Burlington are either an 11 or a combination of numbers that add up to the number 11.

Below: At the top of this building, the occult seeker will find the torch of the eternal flame. Eternal flames most often commemorate a person or event of national significance or serve as a reminder of commitment to a common goal.

church, stated the following in the *Journal of Discourses*, volume 19: "The dead will be after you, they will seek after you as they have after us in St. George (temple). They called upon us, knowing that we held the keys and power to redeem them. I will here say before closing, those two weeks before I left St. George, the spirits of the dead gathered around me, wanting to know why we did not redeem them."

It is quite common to hear Mormon stories about the dead coming to the living and spirit beings being seen in their temples. Stories are told of auras and lights seen around speakers and melodious music being circulated.

SYMBOLIC MAGIC

While walking about the historic district of Burlington, I suggest taking a second look at the architectural designs and symbolism found on its buildings—old and new alike. By doing so, you will find evidence that the occult is alive, well and flourishing in what some would have you think is just another quiet little midwestern town known only for the Nestle Chocolate Factory outside its city limits.

Unknown to most people is a very powerful type of magic that is practiced through symbols called symbology magic. Since those who look for them can find these occult symbols on most of the buildings in the historical district of Burlington, I can only conclude that the founding fathers and builders of this town not only were aware of the meanings behind the symbols and the magic that derives from them but were also using symbology magic for reasons only known to them and those who inherited their secrets. Through time, the practice of this type of magic has been carried on in Burlington, and the people, merely by gazing on the symbols, are being affected, knowingly or unknowingly.

Symbols have always been employed to communicate hidden mystical messages, but for the practitioners of the occult, these symbols are tools specifically used in wielding supernatural powers and communicating their various doctrines. These symbols can be many centuries old, yet their meanings and power remain the same. Although today the observer may not know their meanings, this in no way negates their significance. In *Lectures of Ancient Philosophy*, Manly P. Hall, one of the most influential occultists of the last century, wrote this of symbols: "They are centers of a mighty force and figures predominately with an awful power."

The visitor to Burlington, interested in occult symbology, can find this Eastern Star etched over the entrance of Burlington's Masonic Lodge.

While studying the occult symbols of Burlington, I found the pentagram engraved and used over the entrance of its Masonic temple. A pentagram, while usually given a bad rap by Christians, is a five-pointed star made of five connected lines. This figure is the time-honored symbol of the magical arts. According to Wikipedia, Heinrich Cornelius Agrippa and others perpetuated the pentagram as a magic symbol, attributing the five neoplatonic elements to the five points. If you find the single point of the star pointing upward, it signifies there is a spirit presiding over the four elements of matter and is essentially considered "good." However, according to writer Eliphas Levi, when the single point is pointing down, it signifies evil. Franz Hartmann, author of *Magic, White and Black: or, The Science of Finite and Infinite Life, Containing Practical Hints for Students of Occultism*, agreed: "Let us keep the figure of the Five-pointed Star always upright, with the topmost triangle pointing to heaven, for it is the seat of wisdom, and if the figure is reversed, perversion and evil will be the result."

The Strangite Mormons had this brass plaque made to commemorate Prophet Strang's discovery of the Voree Brass Plates, evidencing what they believed to be an ancient mining community owned and operated by one of the lost tribes of Israel.

This Mormon house, with a historical marker in front, sits across from the area where the brass plates were found.

This photo is of Prophet Strang's home, where he died of a fatal gunshot wound.

Levi goes on to say that a reversed pentagram, with two points projecting upward, is a sign of antagonism and fatality. It attracts sinister forces because it overturns the proper order of things and demonstrates the triumph of matter over spirit. It is the goat of black magic and lust "attacking the heavens with its horns."

The Mormons believe that the Burlington area is the "Promised Land"—the place that Jesus Christ will return to during the End Days. It is one of the sacred places their people are to gather during that time.

CHAPTER 9

UNDERGROUND TUNNELS, GHOSTS AND STRANGE THINGS THAT GO BUMP IN THE NIGHT

BURLINGTON HOSPITAL

While Brad was at the hospital, undergoing some occupational therapy for a work injury, he saw a small, serpent-like light, which appeared to be approximately two feet in length and about two inches wide and emitted a yellow color. The ghostly entity was floating just above the floor, traveling back and forth from the occupational therapy examination room into the bathroom and then back out in the room and going under the table. Soon after, it came back out from under the table and went back into the bathroom. Curious as to what he had just seen, Brad asked several of the nurses who were also in the room if they had noticed any hauntings or strange paranormal activities in the room. One of the nurses responded with a no, but when Brad told them what he had just seen, the second nurse exclaimed to the first, "I told you this place was haunted!" She then shared with Brad that she had noticed a lot of activity going on in the emergency room but felt uncomfortable sharing it with the others. Personally, I would have found it even stranger—with all the high energy that occurs in emergency rooms, including deaths—if there was no paranormal activity.

We mapped out three underground tunnels running under the road connecting these buildings, including an underground bowling alley that we believe was constructed during the Prohibition days. The entrance to the bowling alley has been sealed. Prior to its being sealed, I was able to get some photographs of it.

ROCK'N FUN MUSIC: GHOSTS AND UNDERGROUND TUNNELS

The building located at 549 North Pine Street was where we first started our business, then a doll and collectible shop. We moved from there about seven years ago, and it is now being occupied by Rock'n Fun Records. It was because of this building and the severity of the hauntings we experienced there that I started our Paranormal Research Center. Sometimes, ghosts leave with the occupants, but after speaking to Kelly, the lady who runs the business there, I believe the building is still experiencing hauntings. Kelly reports that most of the activity is limited to the basement area, where an underground tunnel is located. After I spoke with another lady who lives in the apartment above Rock'n Fun Records, I concluded that the upstairs area is haunted as well. I have also spoken with several shop owners on both sides of the record shop who claim to have had their share of hauntings. In many cases, it is difficult for me to get stories of hauntings from the actual owners

The Lincoln School in Burlington, formerly Burlington Union School, was constructed in 1859.

This is the home of abolitionist Dr. Edward G. Dyer, who orchestrated the Underground Railroad in Burlington.

of businesses, fearing these types of stories could be detrimental to their businesses. On the opposite side of the coin, there are other businesses that love to share their stories with the public in hopes that it pulls more business into their establishments.

THE SCI-FI CAFÉ AND RESEARCH CENTER

Located at 532 North Pine Street, this building would have history and many tales to share with us if it could only talk. Built in the 1800s as a hotel, it provided refuge for the weary traveler, including such influential guests as President Grant. As time went on, the hotel lost its glitter and became a house of prostitution. During the Prohibition days, it became what is commonly known as a speakeasy and was frequented by Chicago mobster Al Capone and his gang. It was a popular place to go for the consumption of illegal liquor, gambling and the company of loose women. This building

This large building at 532 North Pine Street was one of the first luxury hotels in Burlington. It now houses the Sci-Fi Café and Research Center on the bottom floor and apartments on the second and third floors. Prior to a proper facility being built, the basement was used to store corpses until their burial.

The Sci-Fi Café and Research Center is known not only for its food and drinks but also for the many ghosts that make this place their home.

had access to the underground tunnels of Burlington, which connected to more underground tunnels running as far south of Chicago as Florida and as far north of Chicago as Moose Jaw, Canada, according to some sources. Capone used these tunnels as a safe passageway for the distribution of his illegally imported liquor. These tunnels were also rumored to have been Capone's dumping grounds for dead bodies.

After leaving 549 North Pine Street and moving into 532 North Pine Street, I could still hear the voices of the small child and mother that I commonly heard in our previous location of the business. For a period of time, I could not understand how this could be. Then we discovered an underground tunnel system that connected the Sci-Fi Café and Research Center at 532 North Pine to our old building at 549 North Pine. Apparently the tunnel was being used as a conduit that linked the two buildings together as one, thus allowing both the small child and mother to visit us by traveling through the tunnels. They have now made their home in the basement, close to the tunnel entrance.

Left: Alien sitting at bar in Sci-Fi Café: People love coming to the Sci-Fi Café to have their photo taken with alien friends.

Below: This is Kathy holding a tape recorder and singing to the ghost of the little girl who resides in the café. Note the strings of energy around her and a white light over her head. The tape recorder picked up the voice of the mother singing along with Kathy.

Through psychics, paranormal researchers, cameras and EVPs, we have learned a few things about the little girl. Using our tape recorder during a session to contact the little girl, Jessica G. asked her what her name was. Listening to the tape, I could clearly hear Jessica asking the little girl this question, and just as clearly, in a small child's soft voice, we heard her answer: "Mary Sue." Using EVP sessions, we have also learned that she loves having people sing her the song "You Are My Sunshine."

Many of the visitors coming to the café ask to go down into the basement so that they can meet the little girl and her mother and sing her special song.

If you sing the song and bring a tape recorder, don't be surprised to hear Mary Sue's voice on the recorder. She is quite friendly and doesn't appear to mind having her conversations taped.

On one occasion, three of us were down in the basement having an EVP session. One of the women (Kathy) had the tape recorder on and went off into one of the rooms and started singing to the little girl. As she was singing, I picked up on the presence of the mother and mentioned it to the other woman who had stayed with me. I told her that I felt the woman's presence next to Kathy. Although I didn't see her, the voice recorder did give evidence of what I felt. On the tape, we could her Kathy singing the song and the voice of the mother singing the song with Kathy. Needless to say, it was a pretty amazing EVP session. We still have the recorded EVP, and guests to the Sci-Fi Café are welcome to listen to it.

We also have had a lot of success with digital photography at the café.

One great accomplishment was when we were able to photograph Mary Sue's mother. The photo showed her being of average height and medium build with long, braided strawberry-blond hair. We also photographed what we suspect was a caretaker of the building. He is shown as thinly built, less than six feet in height and wearing a large brim black hat and black suit. Both photos are viewable at the café.

Another popular spirit that roams the hall of the café and research center is what the psychics have reported as an Indian chief. According to two separate reports, neither knowing the story of the Indian chief, the chief lingers there due to his anger over the army taking the Indians' land and a battle that took place between the army and his people. Although he doesn't

Photo of Brad standing in front of one of the sealed tunnel entrances in the basement of the café. The café has a portal, and when activated, the molecular structure of the physical body changes. In this photo, Brad is becoming transparent and you can see the background through his body.

This is a moving orb along with a group of spirits in doorway.

raise any havoc, one can feel his stern presence. We have tried on several occasions to cross him over, but he refuses to leave until the problem has been resolved. When checking the history of this particular area, skeletal remains of Native American Indians have been found.

The café also has a Caucasian woman that haunts the women's restroom. She has made so many appearances that some of the women who regularly come to the café insist on having someone go with them into the restroom. She has been not only seen but also heard moving things around and sometimes giving a small sigh. As for me, I could never understand why a ghost would want to haunt a restroom until one day I found a photo of the place when it was the old Burlington Hotel. Exactly where the restroom is today was the office where guests would check in and out while staying there. So I would imagine this woman used to work here as the hotel clerk. She has also been asked to cross over, but she refuses, stating she "likes it here." So we keep flowers in the restroom and a cute teddy bear to keep her company.

The "Whistler" is another spirit that has made his home at the café. I suspect he may have been a bartender who worked here when the building was being utilized as a tavern. Usually around 1:00 a.m. and after, when I am working late, I hear very distinct whistles coming from behind the bar. Sometimes, if that doesn't raise the hair on the back of my neck, he will start tapping his fingers on the bar. I believe that he thought it was bar time and was just trying to get all the customers out so he could clean up. There were many times I would be so frightened that I would cease doing my paperwork, pack up and quickly leave. One evening, a friend, Terri T., had stopped in from Florida to tell me of a UFO sighting she had there. As she was telling her story, I was recording it. After she was finished, I forgot to turn the tape off and told her the story about the Whistler. After Terri left, I decided to listen to the recording and make a physical file of her UFO sighting. As I was listening, I heard whistles on the tape. As I heard this, I immediately knew that the Whistler had been there all along listening to us. Apparently he wanted his whistle heard.

Our most recent discovery of a ghost in the café came quite accidentally when I opened the café and library/museum one evening to a research team that wanted to film a documentary of our ghosts that reside here. To my surprise, in the library, we found a shaman or medicine man that had claimed one of our most comfortable chairs. We discovered him via the special ghost-busting equipment they had with them. We learned who he was and what he wanted by using a psychic and special rods that were given to me by a friend who had passed over several years back. We learned that he liked staying in that room because of my esoteric healing sessions I taught on Thursday nights. Apparently he helps me with these classes. He chose a special chair to sit in and made it quite clear, in no uncertain terms, that he did not want anyone sitting in it, including me. So after that evening, I decided that I would respect his wishes, and the chair forever more will be used only by him—unless, of course, he changes his mind.

Although these spirits are the most popular tenants of the café, there have been many more reported by various visitors and ghost investigators. This, of course, is not surprising considering that when this building was first built, the basement was used for storing bodies of the deceased until the town was able to build something more accommodating. The building was also built on an earthen mound and has several tunnels running underneath it.

Some of the mysteries of the Sci-Fi Café and Research Center were unveiled when I received a letter from Michelle D., whose family previously owned the building. The following is what she wrote to me.

Hi! I came across your website sort of by accident but was really taken aback by what I was reading. My family is from the Burlington area, all of us born and raised at some point in the very building you are located.

Back in the day, that building was owned by Bill Ebbers, and my grandfather Norbert Socha was his good friend and caretaker of that building and all thee apartments in it, as well as what became Sharkey's Bar and the small banquet room across from it.

I remember we had every single Christmas party in that small banquet room every year until my grandparents moved out of that building some years after Bill Ebbers had passed. My grandparents had lived in several of the units upstairs as well as on the main floor of that building. My mom, sister, uncles and lots of the family had lived in that building over the years, in different units, including myself. My uncle David Socha actually lived in that basement for some time when we were little. We could all tell you some odd stories!

I remember being so scared of those tunnels and have periods that are blacked out that I have no memories of from that time. I even used to have nightmares about some of the rooms and spaces down there, even as a young adult. I am now in my thirties and haven't really thought about the place in some time. There is so much history there for my family, good and bad.

Even before my family, that place was full of history. It used to be the Plush House and was frequented by gangsters, and there were even a few hideout rooms in the basement from this era. I remember there were a couple

secret rooms my grandfather had discovered in the basement that I, my sister
and about five of my cousins used to play in.
    We also used to play on the roof (crazy dangerous kids we were). We could
all tell you some scary stories about shadow people by the fire escape stairs.
    The small "secret" rooms, as we called them, are in the basement, not
the tunnels. When you enter the basement on the far end near the fire escape
(around the corner nearest John's Main Event), the first main room you
enter is big. We called it the workshop since that's what Grandpa and
David used it for. As you walk down, toward the front of the building, there
are different rooms on both sides of you where they stored paint and different
maintenance type things as well as storage. If you keep going, there will be
a room that had gray carpeting and some rolled up carpet logs where there
is a grate in the wall and a second in yet another room that had carpet logs.
These large grates can be taken out and behind them are small rooms. You
should be able to see where I and my cousins scribbled with crayons on some
of those walls near the grates.

COACHES BAR AND GRILL

Around the block from the Sci-Fi Café and Research Center was another luxury hotel. Built in the late 1800s, it was known at the Burlington Hotel. It was later used as one of Capone's speakeasies because it had several underground tunnels running through the basement area.

What remains of it today is locally known as Coaches Bar and Grill. When it operated as Coaches, the employees dreaded going down into the basement area, claiming it was haunted. I was curious about the place and got permission from the manager to take some photos. As I reviewed the photos later, I found one photograph that showed a headless woman in a white dress standing in one of the tunnels. Wanting to make sure of what I was looking at, I went back to Coaches and asked the manager if I could take a second look at the basement. As I compared the spot with the photo, I was assured that what I was looking at in the picture was indeed a ghost. Since then, others have gone down there and felt cold spots and a presence of something watching them.

Not only is this building haunted, but it also seems to be cursed. It has seen several large fires, and all of its previous owners have undergone a series of bad luck. Several years ago, the last owner, while driving home

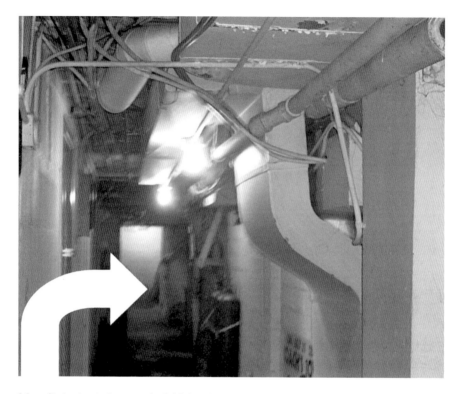

Mary Sutherland photographed this headless ghost standing at end of hall in the basement of Coach's Bar and Grill.

from Coaches, died in a car accident due to a heart attack. The following day, his family locked the doors of the bar and never reopened. Today, it still sits vacant, but if you look through the windows, you will still see the liquor bottles and glasses sitting on the bar, just as he left it years ago.

THE MALT HOUSE THEATER

The Malt House Theater in Burlington, home of the Hay Lofters Community Theater, has a resident ghost that the locals call Esmeralda or the Lady in Blue. Along with Esmeralda, strange things happen, such as seeing lights flicker and go out (and often turn back on when we ask for it) and theater props being moved when no one is around. During a production of *Camelot*, the director unlocked and opened up the theater to find that the candles on stage had been recently lit. It has also been reported that the upper left corner backstage has a cold and clammy feeling, even when the rest of the theater is warm. Esmeralda's personality is described as quite genial, and she is always seen wearing a long, blue Victorian dress. It has been reported that once, when rehearsing a children's show, the kids, knowing nothing of Esmeralda, came in from waiting outside in the area behind the theater to say that a lady in a long blue dress was floating back there.

Some people have reported having sensations of being touched, just to turn around and find no one there. Others have claimed to have experienced a strong presence and the eerie feeling of not being alone in the room. The Malt House Theater is also known to have an underground tunnel. The entrance can be found in a small stone building outside the main building. I have gone there and found it to have several levels. Unfortunately, typical of all the tunnel entrances I have encountered, these entrances were also sealed.

People that either have a business or residence built over these tunnels have reported scuffling sounds and voices behind the tunnel walls. Most, hearing these sounds, assume they are ghosts, and they very well may be. But they could also be of a more physical nature. I have often thought that behind the secrecy of the tunnels, there may be a group that not only knows about the tunnels but is also actively using them for reasons known only to them.

I remember several years back that the Madison Police Department had a severe meth problem. Although they knew that some group was actively distributing meth in the area, they hunted high and low for their labs. Not giving up, they continued their search and finally came upon some tunnels that ran under the city. Breaking through one of the sealed entrances, they ventured into the tunnels and found the source of their problems—meth labs.

Several miles from Burlington is a small town by the name of Rochester that also has underground tunnels running under the streets. One popular haunted place that is known for its underground tunnel is Chances. On the same street as Chances, across the river, the first house on the right-hand side as you cross over the bridge is set up very similar to the Malt House Theater. Brad and I have investigated it and found that this two-story house also has a small stone structure located off to the side of the main building. This stone structure is the entryway to the underground tunnels that we suspect run under the river and connect to Chances. This house is so active that the owner has a very difficult time keeping tenants.

Just like Burlington's Malt House Theater, this house has a small stone building that has steps leading down into a tunnel system running under the river that connects to Chance's Bar and Restaurant, also known for the underground tunnels that run under its establishment and home to a variety of paranormal activities.

Brad Sutherland checks to see if there are any construction workers in the house, but I knew the sound we were hearing was coming from all the spirits that called this place home!

One day, as Brad and I were photographing the house and stone structure, we heard banging and pounding sounds coming from the house. Brad assumed that there was a construction crew inside remodeling the house. As for me, based on what I knew about the house, I seriously doubted his assumption. To prove to me that it was not ghosts, Brad went over to the house and looked through all the windows. He quietly came back to where I was standing and told me there was no one in the house and no signs of any remodeling work being done. If any house made Brad a believer of the paranormal, it was this one. I have also spoken to some of the neighbors, and they told me that, although the house was empty of tenants, it was normal to see strange lights moving about downstairs as well as upstairs.

THE RAINBOW MOTEL

When some of my ghost-hunting friends come into town, I always suggest that they check into the Rainbow Motel. One group spent the night there and did some EVP sessions using their tape recorder. They were quite happy to report that the ghosts were very interactive with them, stating they got on the tape some answers to their questions and a variety of phrases with one stating, "I am sorry."

Others who I have arranged to have a stay at the motel were not quite as pleased. One gentleman reported to me that he was awakened from his sleep by an invisible force grabbing his foot and literally yanking him out of his bed.

Two men from Chicago reported to me that the paranormal activity at the Rainbow was a little too much. One of the gentlemen decided to sleep in his car for the duration of the night after a hideous face manifested in the mirror.

When deciding to spend some time in Burlington, please keep in mind—whether you are staying in the Rainbow Motel or any other motel in this area—you are most likely to experience some kind of paranormal activity.

HILLCREST BED-AND-BREAKFAST

Prior to the refurbishing of this old mansion for a bed-and-breakfast, the locals used to keep their distance, believing it to be haunted. According to several of the locals who grew up in Burlington, when the children walking on the sidewalk to school would get to the property line of what they called the old haunted house, they would run until they got safely past. The former owner of an office supply business here in Burlington told me that her parents owned a house next to the old mansion. She went on to say that one day, their dog got loose and went up to the old house at the top of the hill. She recalled how frightened she was when her folks insisted she go up there to retrieve the dog.

Now that the old haunted house of Burlington has been refurbished, it stands today as a beautiful bed-and-breakfast. The beauty and landscape of the estate entices visitors from around the country to come and spend some time there.

As the old adage goes, however, beauty is only skin deep, and what lies beneath the tranquility of its outer layers is quite different than what the old mansion holds.

The early locals were right in their assumption about the mansion to some extent. There is a very strong energy that emits from this place, which the locals mistakenly thought to be ghosts. The hill that the mansion sits on is not a hill, but a stepped, flat-top pyramid built by an ancient people who once lived here, thought to be the precursors of the Aztec. A common term used today to describe them is Mound Builders. The Native American People, upon coming to this land, described them as being here when they arrived. They called these people the Hu-Kadesh; their population was as thick as the leaves on the trees. They were white-skinned, red-haired giants who stood approximately seven to ten feet tall and were builders of stone.

Researching these people further, I learned that they would build places of worship and pyramids on places of great power, where portals or doorways could be opened to allow their dead ancestors to move from one dimension to another. These places of power were considered to have great magic to them.

Biblically speaking, the bed-and-breakfast was built on a holy mountain and what archaeologists are now referring to as a sacred site.

The locals still pick up eerie feelings as they pass by here because of the multidimensional doorways. Yes, ghosts do come and go as they wish, along with other multidimensional entities.

My conclusion on Hillcrest Bed-and-Breakfast is, similar to what I said before, "beauty is in the eyes of the beholder." Where one could see it as haunted, another could see it as a monument created as a place of worship by our ancient ancestors. I prefer to see Hillcrest Bed-and-Breakfast as the latter.

Sentry Shopping Center

On South Pine Street, across from the local post office is a small shopping center. The tenants who have their business in the center are haunted by a man they have endeared with the name "Mr. Brown." Speaking with the manager (at the time) of the video store, I learned that he was given his name because every time she, along with other employees, had seen him, he was always wearing a brown hat and overcoat. Telling me about Mr. Brown, the manager laughed and told me that he did not like some of the more modern music that they played in the store. She explained that when the employees would play certain music, Mr. Brown would create electrical problems until they put music on that he preferred to listen to. The manager told me that one day, she was alone in the store when she felt someone behind her. As she turned, she saw Mr. Brown dressed in his brown trench coat and hat. He passed her and walked right through a closed glass door. Although he had made numerous appearances at the video shop, none of the employees felt threatened by him. As the manager stated, "Some even came to look forward to their encounters with him!"

This was not the case with the girls who worked at the Salvation Army Thrift Store, a few stores down from the video shop. The girls who worked there told me they were very uncomfortable working alone at the store and were actually terrified to work there at night. Apparently, Mr. Brown liked looking at the clothes on the rack and scaring the pants off the girls. They claimed Mr. Brown would take the clothes off the hangers and throw them on the floor or move the clothes to another place. They also mentioned that he would turn the lights on and off and mess with the sound system that played music throughout the store.

According to the manager of the video shop, the Family Dollar Store right next door has had encounters with Mr. Brown as well. However, I have never had the chance to talk to the girls who work there.

As I tried to investigate Mr. Brown, the closest I ever came to this phenomenon was what author and researcher Heidi Hollis coined the "Hat Man." According to Heidi, the phenomenon of the Hat Man is being reported worldwide. The Heidi Hollis Hat Man, however, is reported to be more like that of a shadow person with ill-intent. The Burlington Hat Man, Mr. Brown, has not shown any of these characteristics. Whoever or whatever Mr. Brown is, we do not know, but we do believe that he is bound to this specific area where the encounters have taken place.

BURLINGTON ACTING SCHOOL

Around the corner from the Sci-Fi Café and Research Center, on Chestnut Street off what is commonly called "the Loop," was an acting school that Coral G. operated several years ago. Even today, due to hauntings and poor luck associated with the building, most tenants have a difficult time making a long run of any business they start up there.

Hearing from some of the locals that I ran a paranormal research center, the owner of the school came to me one evening in hopes that I could help her with hauntings taking place in her school, especially in the basement. That evening, after experiencing a ghostly encounter in her basement, she was so terrified she refused to go home and spent the night on a daybed that I had in my office. Through the weeks, her spending the nights on my daybed became more or less a regular routine for Coral as she waited for me to resolve the problem. Since I worked nights into the wee morning hours, I didn't mind the company, and we eventually became good friends. She even helped me with some of my field research.

Using my camera equipment and voice recorder, I found that, indeed, this building was being haunted, but just confirming her fears would not solve the problem. I needed to find out why it was being haunted and how to release the spirits so they could go on to a more pleasant place than where they were then. What I learned was quite unsettling for me and will be for some of the locals who have always taken pride in the fact that Burlington was one of the towns used as an Underground Railroad stop for freeing slaves.

What I learned was that while Wisconsin was a free state, a few of its residents were making a great deal of money capturing slaves and selling them back to their slave owners. We have found evidence of this in Burlington. Several people have reported to me finding heavy iron shackles hooked to the walls down in sub-basements and tunnel areas of Burlington. In my mind, there would be no other reason for these shackles if it were not for holding people against their will. Being that the shackles and holding areas were found in these subterranean areas suggest to me that this type of practice would not have been looked upon by the citizens as acceptable. Imagine getting as far as Wisconsin and tasting freedom after everything you endured just to be captured and sold back to your former owner. The conditions that these slaves lived in while awaiting their return included near starvation, brutal beatings and unimaginably poor sanitation, with some of the slaves dying. In the case of Coral G.'s building, a group of slaves were being held in the underground quarters when a fire broke out, killing all who were there. We were able to cross over all of them, except for one man. Try as I may, he stubbornly refused to go. Finally, I contacted a very well-known psychic in New York, who did what is called crossover work. She had the ability to leave her body, come to Burlington and speak to the ghost personally. When she did this, she learned of the great fire that took everyone's lives. He told her that he was looking for his daughter, who was also in the fire, and would not leave until he found her. The psychic, using her abilities, found out that the daughter had crossed over upon death. She went back to the father and told him about it, but he would not or could not believe her. Finally, the psychic contacted the daughter and had the daughter come back to this side so that the father could see her. When the father saw his daughter, he broke down in tears and held her tight. The two proceeded to walk into the light together.

What I learned from this is sometimes we misjudge spirits as being evil because they are presenting themselves in an angry manner. We pick up the anger but don't ask why the spirit is showing hostility. After this, I ceased to judge according to the energy I pick up and now try to learn more about the personality. After we crossed over this spirit, Coral G. was able to spend her nights at home and sleep in her own bed without fear.

BUSHNELL PARK

Outside Burlington, at a place the locals call the trestle, thrill seekers go looking for a little ghostly action. From what I have learned from a couple here in town, Jess and Tony, the trestle is located in Bushnell Park. The old railroad tracks have been converted into a pathway, and the railroad trestle has been converted into a walking bridge.

In the wooded area of the park, along the pathway, a female apparition appears. This ghostly form is dressed in white and has become known by the locals as the White Lady. Just prior to her appearance, one picks up the scent of old perfume described as having a musky odor.

Another hot spot in the park is the walking bridge that goes over the river. What is believed to be the ghost of a railroad conductor has been seen numerous times on this bridge. Seen at the park is another apparition that is described as a man in black, wrapped in chains.

The Haunted Painting

Another interesting story witnessed and written by Tina Caskey is about a haunted painting. The following is her report.

It was about fifteen years past that I resided in a house in Burlington, Wisconsin. It was an attic apartment that was quite small but quaint. I had lived there about five years when I met my now husband, Dan. We lived there together quietly until the day that my sister and niece came to stay for a while. They settled into the back bedroom, and it was quite nice having them there with their laughter ringing throughout our home.

One day in the summer, my niece Tiffany went into town to a thrift store called Love Inc. She came home with a museum print of *The Sad Clown* to give to her mother. I, not caring for clowns, pretended to enjoy having it in the apartment though I got the creeps looking at it.

The apartment was fashioned in a circle. When you walked in, you first were in the living room. Directly back and to the left was the spare bedroom, where they were staying. Immediately to the left was the master bedroom. Through there was the bathroom to the right and the kitchen to the left. Going through the kitchen was a slanted ceiling area where I had the dining room table. Then back to the front door. It was a very odd set up.

One afternoon, about two weeks later, I was painting a mural on the wall with the slanted ceiling and had sat down for a bit to look at my progress. As I was sitting there, I saw movement to my right. I turned, and to my surprise and horror, I saw a man coming out of the back bedroom. He was very tall, very old and gaunt and was wearing a black suit with his arms jutting out as if the suit were too small. He was staring at me with such hatred that I nearly screamed. Then, as quickly as he appeared, he turned and walked back into the bedroom. I was frozen and going through my mind were the thoughts, "Did I really just see that? Oh my god, it's the middle of the afternoon; its daytime. What am I going to do?" I stopped staring at the bedroom door when I heard a noise to my left. I turned my head to see, and there was, peeking out from the kitchen, a white figure's head. It was as if a puffy white cloud was staring at me, and then it, too, ducked away. Shocked, I couldn't move.

I stayed where I was—frozen, terrified—for about an hour thinking about what had happened and came to the conclusion that it had to have something to do with the clown painting. And as it came from a thrift store, I knew that it might have had attachments.

Finally my sister came home, and I told her what had happened.

My sister, though she believed me, didn't share my opinion that the spirits came with the clown painting and was adamant that it stay on the bedroom wall. The painting had sentimental value to her, being that her daughter had given it to her. Since I didn't have any proof about the painting's being haunted and understood her sentiment, it remained on the wall.

A few days later, we were all sitting in the living room. My niece was on the chair to my left, I was in a chair with my back to the spare bedroom and my sister was cross-legged on the floor in front of the T.V. Suddenly, my niece said, "Ewwwwwww, what is that nasty smell?" About the time I, too, smelled the scent of rotten cabbage, my sister turned to look at me and screamed. I flew off the chair and crawled over to my sister, whipped around and saw nothing. I asked her what she was screaming about, and she said that that man was right behind my chair. Again he had disappeared as fast as he had appeared. Once again, I said that that painting had to go. Needless to say, it stayed.

My girlfriend who lived downstairs decided to have a psychic come and that we should all have our readings done. After we were through, I asked the psychic to come upstairs and see the mural I had painted. I said nothing about what had happened in the house. She came up with me and looked at the painting and said that it was very powerful and that the room it was in was a place of safety. I thought to myself, you're not kidding and laughed. Then I took her from room to room saving the back bedroom for last. She walked in and immediately looked at the painting and said, "Get it out of here." I asked her why, and she said, "It's bad." So the painting went with me out the door and down the stairs. I put it on the bottom step and stopped to tell my friend what had happened. We were sitting at her kitchen table talking about it when, shockingly enough, a flame shot out from behind her refrigerator! We jumped up to see what had happened and found nothing. No smoke, no flame, nothing. I stood staring at it, and it came to me. I looked at her and said, "Look at this." I opened the door to the bottom landing of the stairs, and there, leaning on the wall that would be behind her refrigerator, was where I had sat that painting.

I grabbed it with chills running up and down my spine and threw it out the door.

When my sister came home, she put it in the trunk of her car, and I haven't seen it since.

The funny thing is I asked her about it, and she looked at me strangely and said, "You know, I had it at Randy's [her ex-husband], and it disappeared. I looked for it everywhere, and it is just gone. I say, good riddance!"

PART II

Multidimensional Worlds

CHAPTER 10
UNSEEN WORLDS AND REALITIES

According to Professor Fred Alan Wolf in *The Spiritual Universe: How Quantum Physics Proves the Existence of the Soul*:

> *As fantastic as it sounds, the new physics called quantum mechanics posits that there exists, side by side with this world, another world, a parallel universe, a duplicate copy that is somehow slightly different yet the same. And not just two parallel worlds, but three, four or even more! In each of these universes, you, I and all the others who live, have lived, will live, and will ever have lived, are alive!*

Dr. Claude Swanson, author of *The Synchronized Universe*, educated as a physicist at MIT and Princeton University, explained to me quite clearly the principle behind the parallel worlds. According to Dr. Swanson, "The synchronization principle leads to the conclusion that all the matter we see is synchronized with our own. There can be many other parallel universes superimposed upon our own, which differ only in the phase or 'frequency of their synchronization.'"

According to quantum physics, energy follows thought, so everything and anything is possible. Whatever you are thinking about or searching for does exist. Whenever an event takes place or a decision is made in which there's a choice of possibilities, the universe splits so that every possibility is realized but in different universes. Can you even begin to imagine the possibilities here? Oops, I just created more universes with just that

Above: This multidimensional portal area was found outside Burlington.

Below: This photo shows a ghostly lion reaching out to wrap a leg and paw around one of the girls.

question! You have also created even more universes by reading this and thinking about the possibilities.

Sometimes these worlds overlap, causing strange phenomena to occur. What we think may be a ghost just may be another person or entity from the other side getting too close to the veil that separates the two realities, causing a projection of a shadowy image. Just as it may surprise and frighten us, it may cause the same reaction from the person living on the other side of the veil. In other words, we may appear as ghosts to them. Physicist Dr. Robert Neal Byrd's research supports me on this, explaining that there is a thin veil that separates the physical world from the astral planes or dimensions. It is not only conceivable that we are experiencing interaction but the higher dimensional spaces are also having interactions and overlaps. In exploring these dimensional realms, he firmly believes that one should proceed with caution.

VORTICES AND PORTALS

In a vortex area, such as what we have in Burlington, portals are created, which are doorways into these other worlds or dimensions. When this happens, time and space become distorted and a lot of strange things can and do happen. One may step into a doorway leading into another dimension and never notice; at other times, it is quite obvious that you are not in the same place or the same time—and some people have stepped into them never to return.

For approximately fourteen years, through digital photography, Brad and I have been documenting the multidimensional worlds along with the portals and strange entities that live within. We have watched objects appear from out of nothingness and have been photographed many times disappearing through the gateways into the other realms.

When I first started researching the vortices, I only knew what my photos showed me. Now after gaining confidence in my sensitivity, I actually hear and see the vortices along with multidimensional doorways and spirit energies. Today, when I walk through a vortex into a portal, I immediately sense the time and space distortion that has been created.

Walking through my favorite portal area in the woods outside Burlington, I fine-tune my senses to the sounds and smells of the forest. As I walk through the portals, the sounds around me will vary from loud,

Brad is standing here looking at some of his photos while our friends Susie and Jane enjoy themselves portal jumping. Note how Susie is standing at the bottom right while you see her etheric double and Jane up in the trees. Also notice the different facial expressions.

to faint or sometimes completely muted. The area where the sound mutes itself we call the dead zone. It is like walking into a vacuum: the pressure of the air changes, and I will experience a ringing in my ears and a pulsating sensation in my third eye, located above the bridge of the nose at the center of the forehead. I will experience a small headache or my vision will blur. The equilibrium will be off, and I have a tendency to lose my balance or walk like I have had a few too many drinks at the local pub.

In the woods, I and other researchers have experienced time loops where one action is repeated. For example, I may walk by a tree only one time but find myself experiencing a repeat of the event. This always reminds me of the movie *The Matrix*, where the black cat was seen walking up the same stairs twice.

Some portal areas are extremely warm, causing those who walk through them to experience an increase in body temperature, sometimes to the degree that they break out in a sweat. Other portals seem to have the opposite effect, causing the experiencer to feel quite chilled.

Emotions and judgment are also affected. We have observed people walking in the portal areas showing a range of emotions, from exhilaration to quiet and melancholy. Brad's theory is that whatever attitude the person has going into the portal area of the woods becomes intensified. I also believe that a person's attitude will draw like spirits around them. Thus, negative will attract negative, and positive will attract positive. So my suggestion is to stay out of these areas if you are depressed or angry or if you have been drinking.

We have also noticed that the oxygen level drops, causing many people to yawn as they walk through the area. While some are experiencing exhilaration from high energy, there are others who come out of the woods just the opposite, feeling tired and drained of energy. For those, I always suggest taking a warm to hot bath with one or more cups of Epsom salt in the water when they get home. Relax, drink a glass of red wine and allow the salt in the water to rid the body of any negative energy it may have absorbed while in the vortex area.

In this photo, you can find various dimensional entities that look like monkeys hiding in the portals above the group members' heads.

I and others have entered these realms quite successfully, but it is wise for the dimensional explorer to proceed with caution and always keep in mind the possibilities of not returning.

While some of these portals are permanent, there are others that are unstable, manifesting for only brief moments in time. Although Dr. Byrd finds it conceivable that a person might be able to pass through these doorways, the issue for him is the return path. If the doorway closes while a person is still in there, the trip could become a one-way ride to who knows where!

CHAPTER 11

ORBS, DEVAS, SYLPHS AND OTHER FANCIFUL CREATURES

SPECTRUM OF VISION

Our spectrum of vision is quite limited, so anything with a frequency moving faster than the speed within our spectrum simply becomes invisible to us. Not understanding how the human sight works nor understanding how our reality has been adjusted to a certain frequency, most simply do not know about the entities that interact or live among us. Simply stated, just because we can't see something does not mean it is not there. It simply means we can't see it!

Within this invisible realm, a multitude of life forms not only live but also thrive in all shapes, sizes and agendas. Today, many of us researchers are working to prove the existence of these realities. We are attempting to show you that these worlds are not only real but just as real as the world we live in. I believe that Brad and I have been very successful in providing proof of this world through our digital photography. We now have tens of thousands of photos bearing witness to this invisible realm and the magic contained within it.

BIOFORMS

A pioneer in this field of research is Trevor Constable, who was one of the first to provide photographic evidence of the invisible life forms existing around us. Constable's photographs show us conscious etheric energy forms. He coined "sky creatures or sky fish," known more commonly in the scientific world as bioforms.

In 1957, Constable and Jim Woods traveled to the southwestern desert with infrared photographic equipment in hopes of proving to the scientific world that these sky creatures existed. By mid-1958, they returned with over one hundred anomalous images on film. Some showed dark objects, others showed extraordinary ellipses looking like living cells and still others resembled UFOs.

In 1976, Constable wrote a book titled *The Cosmic Pulse of Life*, which shows six consecutive pictures in which he stands some distance away with his hands raised in the air. Descending into the frame is a clear amoeba-like anomaly that, in a mere quarter second of exposure divides in two then joins back together, before finally ascending out of the frame.

In his book *They Live in the Sky*, Trevor shows huge, plasmid-like living creatures. Constable's daughter has also captured a bioform near a cloudbuster–orgone energy transmitter. The photo taken by Trevor's daughter is very similar to the bioform that Brad was able to photograph floating over a group of people we had taken into the Burlington woods.

Another researcher who was successful in capturing the elusive bioforms on film was the late Luciano Boccone from Genoa, Italy. Using infrared waves, he was able to capture on film long processions of critters flying across the sky. According to Boccone, this fleet of bioforms was drawing energy from a steel production plant. Time-lapse photos show the sky creatures being drawn to street lights, making sharp turns and reversals, materializing and dematerializing.

SYLPHS

My personal favorites are the sylphs. Paracelsus was responsible for giving them the name, describing them as having the shape of a slender young woman. Although they do have a willowy appearance, the sylphs are both male and female. They are immortal and born of the air and ether. They live in the sky and are responsible for the clouds. The typical cirrus and cirronimbus formations are expressions of the sylphs. These sky creatures inhabit the same volume of space as the air, but their actual being resides in the physical vacuum as a coherent holographic form of energy.

During World War II, the sylphs were spooking not only our air force pilots but also the Germans, who gave them the name gremlins. The United States considered them to be a real pest for their pilots and ground crews, as the sylphs prevented their air force from carrying out some of their missions. This became such a problem that the air force began developing ways of detecting and repelling the sylphs. At first, they tried using infrared photography to detect them, but it took too much time to develop the film. They later found and utilized the Royal Rife and Ruth B. Drown instruments, which could instantly detect the sylphs. After detection, microwave and radio frequencies were used to repel them.

Although our military may disagree, the sylphs are very important to our ecosystem. The destruction of the sylphs could destroy life on Earth as we know it. We need not worry too much about this, however, because the sylphs are here for life on this planet and help us on a daily basis.

They have been known to divert weather fronts to help aircraft and people on the ground. The sylphs have done everything possible to prevent nuclear war and have warned pilots away from deadly situations. Although destructive wind and rain happen, if the large weather fronts from the tropics were shut down, the temperate climates worldwide would turn into deserts.

The sylphs are constantly using wind, rain, lightning, thunder and fire to break up concentrations of static or deadly orgone. Unfortunately, because of the chemtrails and electromagnetics from the High Frequency Active Auroral Research Program (HAARP) and the Ground Wave Emergency Network (GWEN), it has become increasingly more difficult for the sylphs to function. (Aluminum particles in the chemtrails are used to get inside sylphs and zap their air gels.)

DEVAS

Another favorite of mine are the devas. The devas have a very important role to play and have been looked at throughout our biblical history as angelic beings. According to R. Ogilvy Crombie, one of the four founding figures of the Findhorn community, the elementals, or nature spirits, use the energy channeled to them by the devas to build up an etheric body or etheric counterpart for each plant, according to its archetypal pattern. Dr. Robert Neal Boyd describes the devas as coming in all kinds of odd shapes, colors and sizes.

ORBS

I believe the most popular photographed evidence we have of life in the invisible realm is in our orb photography. It seems these fellas love making their presence known.

There are many theories as to what orbs are. Some could be spirits of people who have crossed over; others could be elementals or devas. Still others might be artificially created monitors used for viewing life in our three-dimensional planes.

Some researchers believe them to be a race of multidimensional beings. Scientists who have researched orbs believe their bodies are made up of dense groupings of charged particles called plasma. This could mean that orbs are the simplest sentient beings in the universe.

They appear to be polarized to light and seem to express positive feelings of love, happiness, bliss and joy. Their bodies are so fragile and sensitive that they are incapable of processing negative feelings of pain and anger. Just witnessing a conflict can hurt them. Not being able to fully experience "negative or dark" feelings, they are quite innocent in nature. You could say that orbs are like children who never grow up. This, of course, is evident in their bubbly outgoing demeanor and child-like naïveté. They are very playful and inquisitive and love to explore. I have also noticed while photographing orbs that they seem to be greatly attracted to people with positive energy and keep their distance from anyone that is projecting negative energy.

In the summer months, we provide tours to some of Burlington's paranormal hot spots. I must admit that I do take advantage of these tours in hopes of photographing and observing strange light anomalies and paranormal activity surrounding participating members in the group. By doing so, I have observed that if the people on the tour are showing positive emotions, there is an abundance of orbs found later in the photos. These orbs, like children, are all over the group, riding on their backs, shoulders, heads or just tagging along. But if we take a group of people on tour that are expressing negative feelings, the photos show very little orb activity. The orbs that are there seem to hang back to observe. They remain at a distance and are more often than not found high over the people's heads.

Another researcher friend of mine, Kent Steadman, who crossed over several years back, had broken down his thoughts on orbs in the following way:

This photo is of a grouping of orbs in various colors and shapes.

They are real, inter-dimensional vehicles. Known to the Egyptians as sun boats and referred to in the Bible as merkabah. This is not an exaggerated claim. Many people believe that this is part of what God made when he created us. It is where we change into and the vehicle we use to get around after this life. The phenomenon known as an out-of-body experience involves this same aspect of our spiritual makeup—another little-known aspect of our own existence.

Real orbs can be not only sensed but also heard. The sound they make is of a super high-tone pitch and usually is heard beyond normal hearing within the head. Among those who are familiar with real orb contact are accounts of the orb speaking telepathically to them. A good time to look for one is when you sense their presence. They usually appear as a barely visible ball of energy floating near you.

True orbs have different appearances, and more than one type exists. The first type, the human spirit or ghost type, is usually seen at about eye level to ceiling height and is often photographed and filmed in graveyards and "haunted" locations. The human spirit type may appear larger than some of the other types of orbs.

Another type of orb is used in conjunction with electromagnetic vehicles (thought of as UFOs). They serve to assist and shield the beings inside the craft as well as be used as a means of propulsion. They primarily are seen high up in the sky, higher than the human spirit orbs, although they are, on occasion, also seen at eye level. This is believed to be due to their higher dimensional level of existence. These are the fully visible orbs seen in photos and videos we will share that are capable of invisibility and extremely high-speed flight.

Another form of orb known to us is considered to be a spiritual aspect of the ET visitors, much like the human spirit orbs are an aspect of us. They often have a more detailed and complex appearances, which can at times contain figures and or faces.

CHAPTER 12

COMMUNICATING WITH THE SPIRIT WORLD

The unconscious mind possesses the facility of receiving from and hence living in a number of universes. Since, physical signals cannot pass from one universe to another; we must assume that the unconscious mind is a non-physical communicating with the physical.
—Birkbeck College, University of London

Since an infinite number of universes contain the physical body of a given individual, one might suppose that if telepathy exists, then some telepathic communication could be possible between at least some of the minds corresponding to those bodies. These communications would be equivalent to receiving signals from another universe.

Some branches in the scientific world theorize that boundaries, or veils, could exist between local dimensional universes and that certain minds are capable of transmitting or receiving signals from several universes simultaneously, all the time unaware that they are doing so. Telepathically, these minds can make contact with and instruct the minds of witnesses to receive these signals—their perception will follow suit.

In John 1:1, it is stated that something called "the Word" is identical with our creator: "In the beginning was the Word, and the Word was with God, and the Word was God." The Vedas call this *Anahad*, which means unlimited sound. When one quiets his soul so that he can hear the divine voice, he is relieved from all worries, anxieties, sorrow, fear and disease. The soul of the listener becomes the all-pervading consciousness.

In my book *Living in the Light: Truths Revealed*, I refer to the word as the audible life stream, the living word of the creator. In this concept, we are all part of a collective consciousness, which makes up the body of the creator—it is our direct line to the universal consciousness. It can be explained like electromagnetic radio waves that fill all space of the cosmic universe. These waves are being transmitted to us, and all we need to do is learn how to tune our receiver to their frequencies.

Although the terminology is different in quantum physics, the principles are the same, adding support to the presence of the audible life stream. The essence of our universe is composed of a systematic and synchronized pattern of which we are all part. We are a subatomic particle, existing both here and someplace else, at the very same time—all connected within the same pattern or reality. Quantum physics shows us that an observer cannot observe without altering what he sees. Through focus or the conscious will of thought, we can use invisible vibrating energies or waves, consisting of subatomic particles, to create our desires to manifest into the physical world.

Carl Jung coined the term synchronicity and stood by his belief that the phenomenon of synchronicity shows us that there is no such thing as a random act or coincidence. Jung reported that synchronicity consists of the universal energies that are invisible vibrating waves similar to radio waves.

Through the audible life stream, we not only pick up on cosmic and universal events but also consciously or subconsciously transmit and receive messages and emotions of others. We can also, through our thought patterns, create events. Everyone, at some time, has experienced this phenomenon. Examples could be explained as being at the right place at the right time. You were thinking of someone, and when the telephone rings, it is that person on the other line. Examples of synchronization are endless.

When properly instructed or guided, we are able to have a conscious communication with the entire cosmos. Upon accepting synchronization in your life, you will learn how to go with what we call the flow. The flow is a natural and effortless unfolding of our lives in a way that moves us toward wholeness and harmony.

When we are in the flow, occurrences line up, events fall into place and obstacles melt away. It is a time when we feel we are in the right place, at the right time, doing the right things. To have the flow properly work for you, you need to learn how to read the signs and allow them to guide you in your life. Signs could be as insignificant as a bird flying in front of you, a book being dropped in front of a store or a leaf falling and landing in your lap. Flow works according to our beliefs, behaviors and actions. When you are open, willing and trusting, you will experience the flow as fulfillment and joy with frequent occurrences of synchronicity. If you are fearful, doubtful and controlling, the flow diminishes, and your life path becomes full of obstacles and frustration with synchronicity decreasing.

We are the microcosm of the universe, all existing as cells within the entire body of the cosmos, harmoniously working together as one single unit. We have been put together, organized and adjusted to share and correspond to everything within this universe. By understanding the working mechanics of your body, you will then become closer to understanding the mechanics of the cosmic intelligence. Because of our creation, we are able to communicate our thoughts throughout the universe as well as use these thoughts to co-create.

Between synchronization and intuition lies a fine line. Although they almost seem to be the same, they are two separate phenomena. In comparing the two, keep in mind that synchronicity is external—it is out there, against the odds, but seems to swing into place to help answer our inner needs. Intuition is internal—it is our inner knowing, our ability to tune in to knowledge in a nonrational and nonlinear way. *We know something but just don't know how we know it.* But in both cases, it shows us just how much our life is interwoven with everything within the cosmic intelligence and that we live in a world more intricately and holistically organized than we could have ever imagined.

As the first party (in the 3rd dimensional world) observes the second party (in another multidimensional world or vice versa), energy between the two parties is transmitted. When the two transmissions of energy come together in the middle, a bubble or "orb" filled with information is created which can then be shared by both parties. Through this simple process, we pick up not only the thoughts and images of the object or being we are observing but also its emotions, and the object we are observing is doing the same thing with us.

RELAYING MESSAGES THROUGH OBJECTS

The Cherokees used the stars as relays for messages between different bands in war and hunting parties. They would decide before they went out at night which star they were going to use. After the hunting party split up into smaller bands, members of the different groups would put their attention on that star and send or receive a mental image accompanied by emotions. This method worked exceedingly well. The star they selected could have been hundreds or thousands of light years away, yet their messages were sent and received in real time. One of the bands could send a message to the star, and another could pick it up any time after that. During the day, they would select a mountain to use as a relay, which they claimed worked as well.

TULPOIDS

In the summer of 2005, while dowsing at Bohner's Lake with my researcher friend Jolene, I pulled a tulpoid from the mind world into our physical world. I was able to do so by connecting my physical mind to the mind world of the unphysical through the act of dowsing. Dowsing has been used since ancient times to help the mind achieve a state of full concentration and stability for the purpose of connecting to the divine conscious that is connected to everything and everyone in both the seen and unseen worlds.

Here is a photo of a scorpion tulpoid that manifested on my face as I was dowsing for information from the spirit world.

When I was able to make full connection, an ethereal-type scorpion appeared on my left cheek with its tail extending downwards to my neck and then back up around my ear. Although it could not be physically seen, the tulpoid was quite viewable on the photo my researcher friend Jolene took and on the camera's viewfinder.

Physicist Tom Bearden, author of *The Excalibur Briefing*, explains that the mind world and the physical world share the same time dimension. Dynamic movements in each world (mind and matter) result in an exceedingly small cross-talk being projected into the other world. This cross-talk is so small as to be virtual and *normally* immeasurable. Establishing one-to-one cross-talk from the mind world constitutes the creation of the tulpoid.

Because I was the experiencer and not the scientist, I sent a photo of me with the scorpion on my cheek to Dr. Robert Neal Boyd along with my explanation of the events that took place. His answer that came back to me confirmed my suspicions: "It may be a tulpoid, which, in the Tibetan Buddhist tradition, is a mind-originated creation manifesting in visible form." He followed up by warning me, "Remember, the human mind, coupled with consciousness, is a powerful thing and must be watched carefully as to what it is creating or de-creating."

Intuition

To become "psychically aware" is simply a matter of perception that is activated by using your nervous-muscular system and the five senses of sight, hearing, touch, smell and taste.

Heightened perception comes when you become "aware" of your environment, making it easy to note the subtle changes that are going on around you. It is seeing not just an object and its immediate surroundings, but the contouring, shading and variations in color, sound, taste and smell that give us a better appreciation of what we see.

In the next few minutes after asking your higher self (higher consciousness) for help on a subject, take note on how you feel. What are you thinking? What tastes do you have in your mouth? What are you smelling and what do you first see when you open your eyes?

Another tip I have is to write down the first thing that comes to mind when you think of a place, person, color, time, town, river, food, weapon, fear, memory, etc. You can write each of these on a card and go through them to get immediate answers; do each one quickly, and if you do not get an answer then make one up.

When ready, be fully aware of your environment, ask your question and then note all the changes to your environment. Note a memory of a person or situation that comes to mind, a change of taste in your mouth, the shivers, a funny smell, hearing a noise that you did not notice before or a picture flashing into your mind.

As your psychic awareness develops, you may walk down the street and notice a particular color, shape or object. You may perhaps notice that rocks or certain flowers in a garden seem to call out to you, or you may find yourself attracted to something in one of the local shop's windows. All these things were there before, but now your newfound awareness is drawing your attention to them—possibly to give you a message.

I have found that when you seek guidance on a situation, sometimes a memory of a person or an event comes to mind. The relationship with that person and the events surrounding the event may be indicators as to how to resolve your present situation.

Sometimes, it helps to ask for further clarification, and a thought may pop into your mind. Now, that first thought is intuition coming from your right brain. Any thoughts after that are in most likely coming from the logical, or left, brain, which is not based off intuition.

Record your thoughts and experiences. Keep in mind that each person has their own pattern on how intuition works for them. For one person, smells may be more prominent, or mental images might be to another. Other people may pick up on symbols, numbers, dreams, visions or events, faces of people, etc. By recording these, you will soon find your own pattern for psychic intuition.

Your Thoughts Make a Difference

Quantum physics shows us that all atoms, cells, molecules, plants, animals and humans participate in a flowing web of information. Physicists have shown that if two photons are separated, no matter by how far, a change in one creates a simultaneous change in the other. Through this observance, it would also indicate that one individual's thoughts and actions, being one living cell within the universal body, would have a direct influence on the whole. In the book *The Hundredth Monkey*, Ken

Keyes also presents how each of us affected the whole unit. The book notes that in a span of thirty years, Japanese scientists observed a group of Japanese snow monkeys. One monkey within the group began washing a sweet potato in a particular way in the salt water. Soon, many of the younger monkeys began mimicking this deed. That observance in itself was not to be claimed as unusual, but after a certain number of these monkeys continued to act out this new washing pattern, the same behavioral pattern developed in another group of monkeys hundreds of miles away. While some may disbelieve Ken's book as to its authenticity, I have found the concepts of morphogenetic fields and critical mass to be true, and the story serves to illustrate this phenomenon.

It has been theorized that once a critical mass number is reached, the same behavior begins to appear in all of the other members of that same species. Physicists describe it as a phase transition, theorizing that when the molecules of atoms align in a certain way and a critical mass number is reached, the rest of the atoms spontaneously line up the same way. This invisible force applies not only to animals but also to plants, insects and everything in the cosmos. Scientists have reported that when liquid matter crystallizes on one part of the planet, the same process occurs almost simultaneously in another, without physical contact.

ELVEN CURRENTS

When our thoughts make contact with thoughts coming from another universe, the energy or light is intensified, creating elven currents. When this inter-dimensional communication is being exchanged from one universe to another, we can capture, on camera, a charge of energy that looks like small bolts of lightning. Dr. Robert Neil Boyd explains the area where the charges are being created as "paradigm symbiosis and interaction." This space formed that enables the flow or exchange of information, meaning, a space is formed that enables the flow or exchange of information coming from different universes. It is an area of interplay between forces, so much so that one could think of that space between the interacting charges as also having a force of its own.

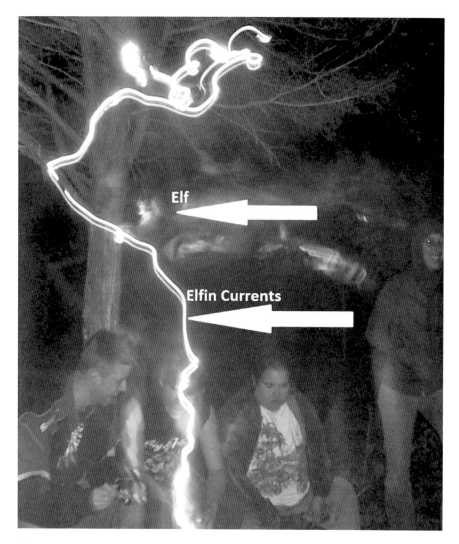

This is a photo taken by me of elven currents, and if you look closely, you will see an elf up in the tree.

APPORTATION

Although this happened to me in Arizona, I wanted to share another form of communication and phenomenon called apportation.

The first experience I had was in the 1980s while living in Apache Junction. This area is in the Superstition Mountains, which have always been known for their vortices and mysteries.

One night, while my now ex-husband was on a business trip, I went to bed and pulled my two children in with me. The bed was situated with the head up against the bedroom window.

I awoke to a roaring sound so loud I thought a train was coming right through the house. As I jumped up, I noticed the bedroom curtains were being blown straight out, like there was a strong wind coming through the window. As soon as I sat up, the sound immediately ceased and the curtains dropped back to their normal position. I looked out the window, thinking maybe a tornado went through, but the night was quiet with not a breeze to be felt. As I was trying to figure out what the heck had just happened, I felt a throbbing sensation in my hand. I looked down at my hand and noticed that I was clenching my fist. I was clenching so hard that my fingernails were cutting into my palm area. As I unclenched my hand, I found that I was holding on to a small white stone. I thought to myself, "How in the world did that get in my hand? It sure wasn't there when I went to bed."

At that very moment, I heard a voice in my head, saying to me, "You brought the rock back, so that you would never forget where you were."

At the same moment, a vision came over me, showing me that I had been in a place with a very large library supported by tall round marble pillars. I was shown several large rooms with people either walking around with books and scrolls in their arms or sitting at marble tables studying. The people were dressed in some sort of white linen material, draped over their bodies, which reminded me of Grecian attire.

I saw myself standing in a hall that was located off one of the larger rooms. On both sides of this hall were high shelves stacked with books and scrolls. As I was seeing this vision, I again heard the voice. This time it told me, "This is the Great Hall of Learning."

I looked at my children, who were by now wide awake, and showed them the rock. I asked them to never forget what happened that night.

Some friends came over to visit me the next morning, and I showed them the rock, explaining what happened. One of them examined the stone with a loop. He exclaimed that the stone was indeed special. It was white crystal quartz with small veins of both silver and gold running through it. Now, I don't know how familiar any of you are with gold and silver, but while they can both be found in quartz, having both in white quartz is highly unusual.

I decided to get it further analyzed by taking it to a rock shop in Apache Junction that specialized in gold and precious stones. Since I wanted witnesses to what I found out, I had my friends go along with me. The owner confirmed what my friends had told me.

For years, I questioned people as to what the Great Hall of Learning was or where it could be located. It was only after I came to Burlington that I found the answer to my questions.

The answer came through my discovery of the works of Edgar Cayce and Sylvia Browne. The Great Hall of Learning was, according to Cayce and Browne, the Great Hall of Wisdom. Although the name was slightly different, the description of where I had been was identical to Cayce's description. Not only did I now have a name for the place I had gone, but I also had an understanding of how I was able to go. According to Cayce, I had experienced the phenomenon of astral travel.

Now, after all these years, two-thirds of the mystery had been solved. But I still had to ask how I managed to pull something physical back from the astral into the physical world. To me, this seemed impossible. The only reference to such a phenomenon was something I saw later on a movie called *Nightmare on Elm Street*, where the heroine of the show, pulled Freddy Kruger's hat out of her dream.

Two years ago, a friend finally helped me to solve the final mystery. Although he didn't know anything about the phenomenon, he did have a name for it: apportation.

Now that I finally had a name, I began surfing the Internet for anything I could find on it. Even on the web, I found very little information on apportation, but through perseverance, I finally managed to find what I was looking for.

The following information is what I have on this phenomenon:

1) Vortices are the result of a tremendous circulatory energy phase out. The phase out is responsible for a certain revolution of a cycle that produces manifestations. When the rings in the vortex have been charged, they allow clarity of the picture to be manifested.

2) The entities of pure light and those that have gone through a long period, or phase, of being restructured themselves are the only ones that can materialize in this. Whenever you are going into a vortex of this kind, the person experiences a strong grounding process. Within the energy field is a spiral. If you are not grounded properly, you may come back desensitized and imbalanced. This can be seen as unannounced colored lights appearing in your field from purple to red to also yellow and white. Sometimes what happens is that these lights are so excessive that you will see them come into your house. They would be hovering either around the head area of a person or his or her solar plexus.

3) There are certain kinds of grounding stones that are produced from these effects. These stones appear from nowhere and are called apports, or materializations. These stones provide the traveler a protection as well. They come from an instrument of sorts that is created from the spiraling effect of that kind of rapid energy that is given off while you are in apportation. This instrument of sorts contains a very strong solar plexus content of microwaves that create the stones used for protection as well as healing later.

These stones are referred to as "earth gifts," which also come from another world plane. The contents of the earth gifts are from the makeup of the soil and environment of the other world, which are similar but not the same as the earth plane.

4) Although not designed for spiritual growth, the manifestation produced by apportation does reveal to us the "Manifestation of the Spirit" (as quantum theory speaks to the creation of matter out of nothing, the Bible substantiates the creation of matter out of nothing as well, most notably at II Kings 4:1–7, in which empty jar after empty jar is filled with oil from one jar, and John 6:1–13, in which from four loaves of bread and a few fish, thousands upon thousands of people are fed).

5) The Bible refers to this phenomenon as the "Manifestation of the Kingdom Within." Everyone has what is called a point of personal manifestation within them, showing them who they are and where they are from. When they reach that strong blending of the spirit within and themselves, this manifestation appears, proving to them that they have just entered the "Kingdom Within."

To further comment on the previous paragraphs, I would like to add the following information:

"I awoke to a roaring sound…" I found out later, through my research, that the sound of the astral body coming back into the body can make a loud roaring sound like that of a train or loud cracking sound. (You may have noticed that sometimes, just before you fall into a sleep, you hear a loud crack. That is your astral body leaving the physical barrier, which will sound similar to something breaking the sound barrier)

"…I noticed the bedroom curtains were being blown straight out, like there was a strong wind coming through the window." I again learned this was not wind at all, but my astral-self coming back at such a strong momentum it drew the curtains with it, like that of wind blowing through the window.

Just like Burlington, the Superstition Mountains are known for their vortices. The vortices in the Sups have even stranger phenomena than the ones in Sedona, Arizona. The reason for this is that the Superstitions lie on the same parallel (extreme northern edge, 33° 24´) as that of the Devil's Triangle.

"The entities of pure light… are the only ones that can materialize in this." During the time of the apportation, I was undergoing hypnosis therapy. The first was past and future life hypnosis. Then I went through the process of shedding myself of all my past inhibitions with the final sessions undergoing extensive spiritual cleansing. So at the time of the apportation, you could say my energies were as pure as one could get in this physical life.

Many people have stated that meditation opens the gate to astral travel; however, this was not the case for me. Mine was a dream experience of sorts. I did nothing to promote the idea before I went to sleep. As a matter of fact, I didn't even know such things existed then. What I think happened with me was a combination of events: my cleansing, my desire to find my spiritual source and the vortex.

FAIRIES

Yes, fairies are real and can be photographed. It is much easier to photograph them during the nighttime hours. If they want to be seen, the fairies will illuminate themselves. Their little illuminated bodies can be captured on camera. Daytime photography of fairies is much more difficult. During the day, they camouflage themselves so well most people walk right by them without seeing them. They also have the ability to shape-shift, preferring to be seen as butterflies and dragonflies.

Fairy-watching in Burlington has become a tradition of sorts. It is not uncommon to go into the woods of Burlington and find glittery objects and sweets left for the little people and the fairies.

Every Saturday evening during the warmer months of the year, we take people out into the woods of Burlington to experience fairies. We never walk into the woods empty handed, but carry with us M&Ms. Approximately ten feet into the woods on the left side is the opening to a fairy kingdom. It is here at this location that everyone is expected to leave their candy. Fairies love sweets, and after approximately fourteen years of this tradition, these little elementals fully expect to harvest their treats when I bring a group in. With this offering, the fairy people, in return, open the dimensional worlds of the woods for all to enjoy. However, never underestimate their temperament. They can become quite hostile if you forget to leave a little morsel for them, and they have an excellent memory and will remember who left treats and who did not. It would not be surprising to be pelted by hickory nuts from an unseen source if you did not leave a treat.

Kathy O. Encounters the Wrath of the Fairies

The suggestion and warning I give the reader reminds me of a story of what happened to one lady who did not heed my advice.

One summer day, Kathy O., a friend of mine, went with me into the woods. Being a person who follows her own path and has her own set ideas on how things should be, she decided that the fairies should not have sweets; instead, she brought nuts and fruits for them as an offering. I had told her earlier that I did not think this was a good idea. When we got to the fairy kingdom, I left my M&Ms and stepped back for Kathy to enter. Just as she set down her plate of healthy goodies, we heard a large snap from a tree overhead. A branch had been broken off the tree and was dropped down on the back of Kathy's shoulders so hard that it dropped the poor girl to her knees. She got up and backed out of there as quickly as possible with a shocked look on her face. As she looked at me, I couldn't help but laugh with an "I told you so." Since her lesson from the fairy people, Kathy has never left healthy food again. She now only leaves M&Ms!

Dr. Robert Neil Boyd refers to the little people as the "Almost Here Beings." Boyd states:

> *The little people are normally invisible to human sight. Many of them have their Being in part in another dimension, or reality, slightly removed from ours. This reality is right next door to ours, in fact, touching ours. So I call them the "Almost Here People."*
>
> *In some locations, there is overlapping of these neighboring realities, which make the Little People readily apparent to the normal human visual faculty. If such a location is in your vicinity, it is highly recommended that you spend some time there. Because in these places, not only will you see the Little People, but you may well encounter many of the other supposedly mythological creatures as well.*

Being Taken into the Land of the Fairies

We have all heard the stories of the fairy people taking humans into their fairy world, but most people of the western culture scoff at the very idea of this. However, with the ability I have to photograph the multidimensional world, we have thousands of photos showing people who have left treats for the fairies becoming transparent and disappearing into their dimension. We have also noticed that in most cases, all those that have been taken into the land of the fairies have virtually no recall of the experience. If I did not have the ability to photograph what had taken place, I sincerely doubt that anyone would have ever known what actions transpire between the humans and fairies. According to legends, time is very different in their world compared to ours. For this reason, I believe that when a human is taken into their world, they could remain there for a very long period of time yet never know in this time that they had ever left. The Cherokees call this time/un-time.

Mainstream science is now starting to recognize that there are worlds within worlds, all separated from one another according to frequencies. Each one of these worlds is as real as the world we are living in. We live in this world because our frequency is synchronized to the frequency of this world and everything in it.

I try to explain to our groups that go into the woods that if they can adjust their frequency to the frequency of the fairy world, they can just as easily enter this world as not. Dimensional worlds are quite similar to the many stations you find on the radio or television. By tuning in, one can pick up a station, and when you are in between stations (or worlds), you pick up nothing but static. In the dimensional world, this static is seen as blurs on your camera. By studying the experiencer, I have found that the more the experiencer fine-tunes into another frequency, the more out of phase he or she becomes with our three-dimensional frequency, eventually becoming transparent or disappearing all together. This observation has become apparent to me by taking thousands of photos of people experiencing such molecular changes.

There have been thousands of claims throughout history of people seeing something and then it disappears before their very eyes. In the terminology of metaphysics, this phenomenon is commonly called phase shifting. According to biblical teachings, Jesus was seen appearing and disappearing in front of a crowd. Paranormal investigators call this materialization and dematerialization while others refer to the phenomena as apportation.

Our reality is held in a vortex that is functioning at the speed of light. It holds all the atoms and molecules within. Using Einstein's equation, David Ash and Peter Hewitt make the argument that since matter and light share a common movement at the speed of light, the vortex that holds our reality must be operating also at this speed. And it is because of the vortex swirling at the speed of light that you can see the objects—trees, another person, the sky, etc.—in this reality or dimension.

They theorize that once the movement of the vortex exceeds the speed of light, then a person or object will enter into "super energy," or a new dimension or world. And in that new dimension, the person or object will be again as solid as we are now in this dimension. The only difference is that in this new dimension, the vortices will be swirling at a speed faster than that of the earth plane. Because we can only see within the spectrum of our own light speed, this person or object would no longer be visible to us, lending an assumption on our part that they are no longer here or no longer exist.

In the case of spirit manifestation, it seems that when the vortices of the spirit's atoms are moving at its new speed, the entity will become invisible to our physical eye. When the spirit wants to materialize, the vortices of the spirit atoms are decreased back to the speed for our spectrum of vision. And when it wants to go back home, it reverses the process.

Ash and Hewitt call this materialization "transubstantiation" to reflect the change in the substance but not the form of the vortex. Through transubstantiation, an intelligence, an etheric, a spirit in the afterlife or an object can materialize or dematerialize.

As Ash and Hewitt correctly point out, dematerialization is not dissolution. It is simply the transfer from one dimension to another, with the body physically materializing once again on the other side.

Fairy Rings or Circles

Legends from around the world tell of fairy rings or fairy circles. They usually appear as a noticeable circle in grass. Many times you will find fungi, especially mushrooms, growing within the ring, but this is not always the case. It has also been observed that animals seem to avoid the circles, not wanting to go around or eat anything near them. (This same phenomenon has also been observed with the mysterious crop circles)

It was commonly thought by our ancestors that within these circles, the fairy whirlwinds would pluck a victim from the earth.

ELVES AND THE LITTLE PEOPLE

Quite different from fairies are the elves or little people. While legends and sightings of the little people are mainly confined to fantasy literature, historical sightings around the world have been relentlessly reported throughout the centuries. Even today, we have numerous sightings of various kinds of miniature humanoid beings.

The majority of legends of elves throughout the world confine these small beings to the deep forest, where they go about their own business, leading a reclusive and mysterious life. But there have been other numerous accounts of observations of the little people that by chance someone walking through the woods has come upon, in most cases, surprising both parties.

Although the sworn testimonies of those who claim to have encountered the little people are still being dismissed as an over active imagination or hallucination, we do have evidence, based on archaeological discoveries, to prove the existence of the little people. One example was the discovery in 1932, of a fourteen-inch-tall mummified body found by gold prospectors in the Pedro Mountains sixty miles southwest of Casper, Wyoming. The mummy was found posed, sitting on a ledge in a small granite cave with its legs crossed and arms folded on its lap. It was described as having a flat nose, a low forehead and a broad, thin-lipped mouth. The mummy was X-rayed and analyzed by the Anthropology Department at Harvard University and was certified as a genuine artifact. Both the Shoshone and Crow Indians, who indigenously inhabit the region where the mummy was found, have legends of the little people in their cultural lore.

In the later 1800s, a British archaeological team uncovered hundreds of tiny flint tools in the Pennine Hills of East Lancashire, all of them no longer than half an inch. These tiny tools included scrapers, borers and crescent-shaped knives. The craftsmanship of the tools was extremely fine. In many cases, a magnifying glass was needed to detect evidences of the flaking process that was used to bring these instruments to a sharp point. Corresponding with the Lancashire find, tiny tools similar to these have been found worldwide, including in Devon and Suffolk, England; Egypt; Africa; Australia; France; Italy; India; and the United States.

In the book *Mad Bear: Spirit, Healing, and the Sacred in the Life of a Native American Medicine Man*, Doug Boyd writes about the indigenous holy man known as Mad Bear who spoke to him about a miniature race of beings whom he called the little people. According to Mad Bear, they evolved

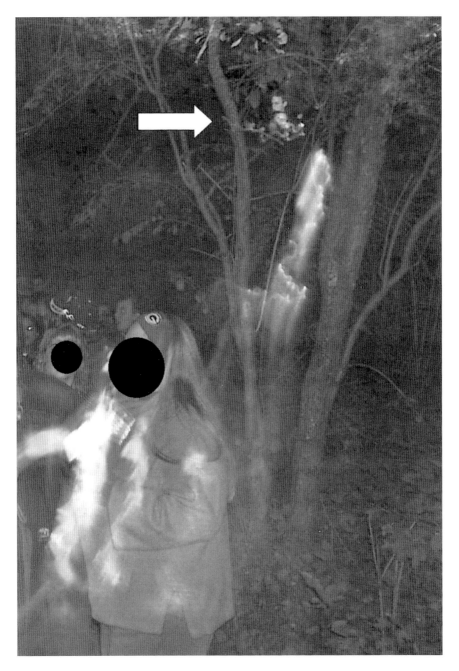

Here is another photo taken by Mary Sutherland of elves hiding up in the tree observing her tour group in the Haunted Woods.

side by side with humans. Mad Bear presented the anthropologist author Doug Boyd with a skull the size of a ping-pong ball to physically prove his thesis.

Having encountered the little people in the Burlington Woods and actually photographing them, I find them quite intriguing, enough so that I did a study on them to find out if they inhabit other areas besides Burlington. Not surprisingly, I found archaeological evidence and lore of them throughout the United States. Following is some of the information I accumulated during my research.

Kentucky

In the 1920s, it is reported that a mummy with red hair measuring three feet tall was found on a ledge in Mammoth Cave, Kentucky.

Ohio

An article in *Gentlemen's Magazine* from 1837 reported that a number of tiny human skeletons from three to four and a half feet tall were found buried in tiny wooden coffins near Cochocton, Ohio. There were no artifacts found, but the number of graves led one observer to note that they must have been tenants of a considerable city.

A short distance from Cochocton, Ohio, a singular ancient burying ground has lately been discovered. According to a writer in *Silliman's Journal*:

> It is situated on one of those elevated, gravelly alluviums, so common on the rivers of the West. From some remains of wood, still apparent in the earth around the bones, the bodies seem all to have been deposited in coffins; and what is still more curious, is the fact that the bodies buried here were generally not more than from three to four and a half feet in length. They are very numerous, and must have been tenants of a considerable city, or their numbers could not have been so great. A large number of graves have been opened, the inmates of which are all of this pygmy race. No metallic articles or utensils have yet been found to throw light on the period or the nation to which they belonged.

Tennessee

The *Anthropological Institute Journal* 6, issue 100, from 1876 gives a report about Pygmy graveyards found in White County and parts of middle Tennessee. One graveyard site was of a vast proportion, giving credence to the stories of a race of little people inhabiting North America. Taken from the report is the following:

> *Some considerable excitement and curiosity took place a few days since, near Hillsboro, Coffee County, on James Brown's farm. A man was ploughing in a field which had been cultivated many years, and ploughed up a man's skull and other bones. After making further examination they found that there were about six acres in the graveyard. They were buried in a sitting or standing position. The bones show that they were a dwarf tribe of people, about three feet high. It is estimated that there were about 75,000 to 100,000 buried there. This shows that this country was inhabited hundreds of years ago.*

While reports are worldwide about races of little people, it was only recently that they were acknowledged by the scientific world through the discovery of a grave site in Indonesia. Following is an Associated Press press release from October 27, 2004:

> *In a breathtaking discovery, scientists working on a remote Indonesian island say they have uncovered the bones of a human dwarf species marooned for eons while modern man rapidly colonized the rest of the planet.*
>
> *One tiny specimen, an adult female measuring about 3 feet tall, is described as "the most extreme" figure to be included in the extended human family. Certainly, she is the shortest.*
>
> *She appears to have lived as recently as 18,000 years ago on the island of Flores, a kind of tropical Lost World populated by giant lizards and miniature elephants.*
>
> *The discovery is the best example of a trove of fragmented bones that account for as many as seven of these primitive individuals. Scientists have named the new species* Homo floresiensis, *or Flores Man. The specimens' ages range from 95,000 to 12,000 years old.*
>
> *The find has astonished anthropologists unlike any in recent memory. Flores Man is a totally new creature that was fundamentally different*

from modern humans. Yet it lived until the threshold of recorded human history, probably crossing paths with the ancestors of today's islanders.

"This finding really does rewrite our knowledge of human evolution," said Chris Stringer, who directs human origins studies at the Natural History Museum in London. "And to have them present less than 20,000 years ago is frankly astonishing."

Flores Man was hardly formidable. His grapefruit-sized brain was about a quarter the size of the brain of our species, Homo sapiens. *It is closer in size to the brains of transitional pre-human species in Africa more than 3 million years ago.*

Yet evidence suggests Flores Man made stone tools, lit fires and organized group hunts for meat.

If you, in your wanderings in nature, happen to encounter some diminutive little people, treat them kindly. Then they'll be nice to you. And when such an event might happen, treat it as an opportunity to discover the wonders of lies "beyond the known."

THE TRICKSTER

Whether it be tricksters, ghosts, fairies, demons, angels, bigfoot, gnomes, elementals, jinn, watchers or aliens, they all seem to bear out common traits—the ability to manipulate time and space and to shift into a shape of which our minds are more willing to accept.

The energy of the tricksters opens us up to the world of limitless possibilities. By creating chaos, old stereotypes—whether they've been imposed by ourselves, our families, our culture or circumstance—are challenged and cultural beliefs reshaped.

While the trickster phenomenon has existed since time began, there is still much debate as to what it is. Mainstream science classifies it as "morphodeception"

Don Juan explains that they are inorganic beings separated from us by a most formidable barrier—energy that moves at a different speed.

Some of the UFO sightings we have today have been theorized as projections of the tricksters in an attempt to help our culture accept the possibilities of civilizations other than the human race. Researching these phenomena, Jacques Vallée concludes: "We have had to note carefully the chameleon-like character of the secondary attributes of the sightings: the shapes of the objects, the appearances of their occupants, their reported statements, vary as a function of the cultural environment into which they are projected."

While most are not comfortable exploring the possibilities of new worlds, dimensions and the beings that live within, our lives will be most certainly enriched and strengthen if we do. The trickster concept challenges us to realize how limited our perceptions are, that things really don't work quite the way we think they do and that the mysteries in life are ever deepening.

Note: In mainstream science, Vallée co-developed the first computerized mapping of Mars for NASA and worked at SRI International on the network information center for the ARPANET, a precursor to the modern Internet. Jacques Fabrice Vallée is also an important figure in the study of unidentified flying objects (UFOs), first noted for a defense of the scientific legitimacy of the extraterrestrial hypothesis and later for promoting the inter-dimensional hypothesis.

CONCLUSION

In virtually all mystical traditions, there exists an intermediate plane of existence populated by a hierarchical order of beings, from higher angels to lower demons. This plane was referred to as the imaginal, or subtle, realm by the French philosopher and mystic Henri Corbin. He considered it an autonomous realm, existing independently of the individual, who could sometimes perceive it through the imaging facility.

The energy and mysticism of the Burlington Vortex provides the student the tools needed to face his or her fears and gain a higher understanding of the hidden mysteries. Whether it is a sighting of a ghost or a run-in with the White Beast of Bohner's Lake, the experience will open your eyes to new unexplained mysteries. Once you have experienced the mysteries of Burlington—regardless if you can show "proof" or not—a door is opened that will lead you down a new path of mystery and wonderment, where fairies, little people, cryptids and other multidimensional beings make their homes. Throw away your fears and skepticism and view Burlington through the eyes of a small child. If you do, you will see and experience Burlington in the way it was meant to be—a place of unexplained, yet undeniable magic and mysteries.

ABOUT THE AUTHOR

 Mary Sutherland is an author and researcher focusing her work on consciousness studies, ancient history and unusual phenomena.

She is a hands-on researcher and the creator of one of the largest websites on the Internet with hundreds of pages providing information on the paranormal, UFOs, ancient races and their cultures, sacred sites, power points of the world, underground tunnels and cave systems, multidimensional worlds, metaphysics, etc.

The governor of Kentucky commissioned her "Kentucky Colonel" for her work on the ancient sites of Kentucky. For the last five years, she has been exploring, mapping and documenting the ancient underwater structures of Rock Lake near Aztalan. For the last fourteen years, she has been documenting the ancient sites around Burlington, Wisconsin.

Truth is her passion. She believes it is through truth that we will break ourselves free of our present entanglements in life. When we become free, we will create our own personal story of the hero's journey suggested by Joseph Campbell.

Visit her website at http://www.burlingtonnews.net.

She and her husband, Brad Sutherland, own and operate the Sci-Fi Café in Burlington. She is also a tour guide in Burlington, giving tours of the haunted woods outside Burlington, historical tours in Burlington and tours of sacred sites not only for Burlington but also throughout

Wisconsin. For more information on her tours, see http://www. burlingtonnews.net/hauntedtours.

OTHER BOOKS WRITTEN BY MARY SUTHERLAND

The Red-Haired Giants: Atlantis in North America
Living in the Light: Believe in the Magic
Revelations: Truths Revealed
Lost in Time: In Search of Ancient Man
Mysteries: Mysteries of Burlington and Southeastern Wisconsin

Contact the author at burlingtonnews@yahoo.com or by phone at (262) 716-8166.

Visit us at
www.historypress.net
....
This title is also available as an e-book